Cator estate map

BECKENHAM

BECKENHAM

Map of Beckenham in 1935

BECKENHAM

Eric R. Inman
&
Nancy Tonkin

Phillimore

1993

Published by
PHILLIMORE AND CO. LTD.,
Shopwyke Manor Barn, Chichester, West Sussex

ISBN 0 85033 885 9

Printed and bound in Great Britain by
BIDDLES LTD.
Guildford, Surrey

*To Robert Borrowman, G. W. Tookey Q.C., and H. Rob. Copeland
whose enthusiasm for the history of Beckenham
has inspired us to write this book.*

Contents

List of Illustrations ix

Acknowledgements xiii

Introduction 1

Chapter I   The Past 3

Chapter II   The Creation of Beckenham Town 14

Chapter III   Beckenham Town 27

Chapter IV   Transport 41

Chapter V   Education 52

Chapter VI   Industry and Commerce 64

Chapter VII   Beckenham at Prayer 76

Chapter VIII   Beckenham at Leisure 88

Chapter IX   Beckenham at War 99

Chapter X   Postwar Beckenham 112

Bibliography 123

Index 125

List of Illustrations

Frontispiece: Map of Beckenham, 1935

1. Boundary post in Summerhill Wood 1
2. Map of Beckenham pre-1850 2
3. Beckenham entry from Domesday Book 3
4. The Old Manor House in the 1870s 4
5. Foxgrove Farm, *c.*1870 4
6. Kelsey Manor, *c.*1900 5
7. The Mansion at Park Langley, *c.*1910 5
8. Kent House, Kent House Road, *c.*1890 7
9. Stone Farm, Wickham Road, *c.*1910 7
10. Old Wood House, St Georges Road, *c.*1905 8
11. *The George Inn* 9
12. Austin's butcher's shop, *c.*1900 9
13. Shortlands farmhouse, *c.*1918 10
14. The rectory 11
15. Clock House, *c.*1895 12
16. John Cator 13
17. Beckenham Place, *c.*1890 13
18. The population of Beckenham 15
19. The *Station Hotel, c.*1905 16
20. Beckenham Grove, *c.*1915 16
21. Ravensbourne Avenue, *c.*1900 17
22. The Avenue, *c.*1900 18
23. Shortlands Estate advertising map, *c.*1870 18
24. Burrell Row, *c.*1870s 19
25. The High Street, *c.*1903 20
26. Albemarle Road, *c.*1905 20
27. Albert Road, *c.*1910 21
28. Birkbeck Road, *c.*1909 21
29. Wickham Way, *c.*1925 22
30. A Coldman House, *c.*1920 22
31. Elmers End shops, *c.*1907 24
32. Langley Road, Elmers End, *c.*1910 24
33. Upper Elmers End Road, *c.*1925 24
34. Eden Way 25
35. Elmers End, early 1900s 25
36. Early view of Davis Estate 26
37. The Cage, Church Hill 27

38.   Map of Crystal Palace grounds, *c*.1860 28
39.   Old fire and police stations, Kelsey Square 29
40.   Bromley Road with bank and Old Manor House, *c*.1909 30
41.   Opening of new Town Hall in 1932 30
42.   The Town Hall, *c*.1935 31
43.   Fire practice at Foxgrove Farm, *c*.1875 32
44.   Motor cycle fire engine 33
45.   Beckenham Cottage Hospital, *c*.1911 34
46.   Stone Park Maternity Hospital 35
47.   Almshouses, pre-1880s 35
48.   Electricity power station, Arthur Road 36
49.   Elmers End cemetery poster 37
50.   The London & Provincial Bank, Rectory Road, *c*.1910 38
51.   Roger's grocers shop and post office, 1869 38
52.   The post office in Albemarle Road, 1897 39
53.   New post office and sorting office, 1897 40
54.   Beckenham station in 1864 42
55.   New Beckenham station, 1993 42
56.   Shortlands' station forecourt, *c*.1914 43
57.   Beckenham Junction and steam train, *c*.1912 44
58.   Penge East station, *c*.1905 44
59.   Kent House station, Barnmead Road 44
60.   Ravensbourne Station, *c*.1900 45
61.   The Beckenham horse bus, early this century 45
62.   A 109 bus outside the parish church in the 1920s 46
63.   Elmers End bus garage, 1937 47
64.   The Batten Specials, *c*.1937 48
65.   Beckenham War Memorial, *c*.1925 49
66.   Beckenham's first roundabout in the early 1930s 49
67.   The Chinese Garage and forecourt , *c*.1920 50
68.   John Pillin's garage 50
69.   Mr. Dineen and Deen's Garage, Croydon Road 51
70.   St James's School next to the church, *c*.1890 53
71.   Churchfields Road School *c*.1910 53
72.   The Technical Institute, *c*.1914 54
73.   County School for Boys, Beckenham and Penge, *c*.1935 55
74.   Miss Fox and the prefects, 1924 56
75.   Lennard Road staff in 1946 56
76.   The Hall in Bromley Road 58
77.   Raymont School, Shortlands, *c*.1910 58
78.   Minshull House, Park Road, *c*.1910 58
79.   Kepplestone School, *c*.1908 59
80.   Advert for a bazaar at Kepplestone, 1905 59
81.   The Abbey School, Southend Road, *c*.1910 60
82.   One of the Abbey School pitches, *c*.1910 60
83.   Clare House School, Oakwood Avenue, *c*.1906 60

84.   Craven College, Dunbar Avenue 61
85.   St Olaf's School, Cedars Road, *c.*1910 62
86.   *The Rising Sun* and Brewery, Upper Elmers End Road 64
87.   Forge in Burnhill Road, *c.*1900 65
88.   Parade of shops at Clockhouse, *c.*1914 66
89.   Hitt's Stores in the High Street, *c.*1904 66
90.   Advertising card for Howard's Stores 67
91.   Sainsbury's in the High Street 68
92.   Parade of shops in Croydon Road, *c.*1939 68
93.   Eden Park shops, *c.*1934 68
94.   Adam's drapery in the High Street, *c.*1910 69
95.   Castle's Nursery in 1920 70
96.   Popham's General Stores on Church Hill, *c.*1920 70
97.   Aerial view of Elmers End in the 1980s 71
98.   Thornton's Corner, *c.*1913 72
99.   A Russell Farm dairy milk-float, 1908 74
100. Holdstock's confectionery and tobacconists, pre-1914 74
101. The church of St George, *c.*1870 76
102. St George's with incomplete tower, *c.*1890 77
103. St George's in 1903 78
104. Lych Gate and bier at St George's 78
105. St Paul's church, New Beckenham, *c.*1905 79
106. St Mary's, Shortlands 79
107. Map showing parish boundaries today 80
108. The Rev. Frederick Chalmers 81
109. Christ Church, Fairfield Road in 1902 82
110. St Michael's and All Angels, Birkbeck estate, *c.*1908 83
111. Bromley Road Methodist church, *c.*1907 84
112. Elm Road Baptist church, *c.*1912 85
113. Croydon Road Mission Hall 86
114. St Benedict's Roman Catholic church, in Overbury Avenue 87
115. Foxgrove cricket pavilion 88
116. Cricket at the Crystal Palace 89
117. Tennis club in Albemarle Road, *c.*1913 89
118. Aerial view of Recreation Ground, *c.*1928 90
119. The Recreation Ground, *c.*1915 91
120. Bowls in Beckenham Recreation Ground, *c.*1906 92
121. Holy Trinity football team, 1905-6 92
122. Golf at Beckenham Place Park 93
123. Crystal Palace Angling Club's pavilion, *c.*1959 93
124. Fishing for tiddlers in Cator Park 94
125. Beckenham flower show, *c.*1910 94
126. Thornton's shop decorated for the Coronation, 1902 95
127. Front of a balloon card, 1902 96
128. Back of a balloon card, 1902 96
129. Elgood playing fields in 1928 96

130.   The Pavilion cinema in the 1920s 97
131.   The Odeon, Elmers End in the 1950s 98
132.   Christ Church Hospital in 1915 100
133.   Balgowan School Military Hospital, *c*.1917 100
134.   Funeral of a Belgian soldier in 1915 101
135.   Oakwood occupied by a transport division in 1915 102
136.   Y.M.C.A. canteen, *c*.1917 102
137.   Beckenham's Peace Parade, 1919 103
138.   Village Place, High Street 103
139.   Shortlands' War Memorial in the 1920s 104
140.   Home Guard inspection at Beckenham Recreation Ground, 1941 105
141.   Auxiliary fire service funeral in 1943 106
142.   Spitfire fund raising appeal at Muirhead's, 1940 107
143.   Café site in Beckenham Road 108
144.   St George's parish church in 1944 108
145.   St Michael's church in 1944 110
146.   Wedding in the church hall in 1950 111
147.   Beckenham Council, 1963-4 112-113
148.   Demolition of the council hall in 1992 114
149.   Beckenham Green in 1993 114
150.   Centenary of the railway, 1956 115
151.   Tesco's during the flood in 1968 116
152.   Sainsbury's in 1963 116
153.   The Beckenham Lace 117
154.   The Beckenham Theatre Centre, 1960 118
155.   *Pygmalion* at the Beckenham Baths in 1949 119

Acknowledgements

A work of this nature would be impossible without the assistance of many people and organisations of whom we would particularly like to mention the following:

Mr. Andrew Hajducki for allowing us to see his unpublished book entitled *The Railways of Beckenham* and permitting us to reproduce an illustration. Mr. A. J. Harris (Beckenham Cemetery and Crematorium) for pointing out the position of graves and allowing us to see the cemetery archives. Mr. Len Hevey for reading the manuscript and his helpful comments. Mrs. J. Inman for proof reading and correcting the manuscript. Mr. A. C. Johns for permission to reproduce illustrations from the Copeland Collection. Mr. R. C. Riley for information and advice on railway matters. The Diocese of Rochester for providing information on the modern parish boundaries. Mr. Mick Scott and the staff of the Bromley Local Studies Library for their help and advice. Mr. Bill Tonkin for help with the computer, photography, and proof reading as well as the continuous refreshments. Mrs. R. S. Tookey for permission to reproduce illustrations from the Tookey Collection.

Inevitably some will have been overlooked. To them we express our apologies and trust the end result will be sufficient compensation for their effort.

Illustration Acknowledgements

Mrs. Joyce Ayling, 71; Beckenham Cemetery, 49; Beckenham Theatre Centre Ltd., 154, 155; Borrowman, 4, 14, 16, 37, 51, 108; British Museum, 127, 128; Mr. R. E. Castle, 95; Cator Estate (Beckenham) Ltd., front endpaper; Christ Church, 109; Copeland Collection; 43, 47, 52, 53, 62; Croydon Advertiser Group, 141; Crystal Palace Foundation, 38; Mrs. V. Davis, 142; Mr. John Gent, 39, 96; Mr. Andrew Hajducki, 18; Miss A. M. Hayes, 70; Mr. Charles Hooper, 140; Hulton Deutsch Collection, 129; Dr. Eric Inman, 1, 2, 55, 90, 107, 148, 149; Mrs. Eileen Jenner, 151; Kent Fire Bridgade Museum, 44; Mr. R. Larg, 50, 115, 124; London Borough of Bromley, 153; London Borough of Bromley Local Studies Library, 23, 46; London Transport Museum, 63; Milne Electrical Collection, Chalk Pits Museum, Amberley, from the *Electrical Review* for January 1901, 48; *Motor Sport,* 64; Muirhead Vatric Components Ltd., 97; Mrs. Irene Mulry, 69; Phillimore & Co. Ltd., 3; Mr. R. C. Riley, 150; Mrs. Olga Roberts, 147; J. Sainsbury plc., 152; St. George's Church, 144; Mr. John Somerville-Meikle, 113; Syndication International, 41; Tookey Collection, 54, 87; Mr. Ray Webb, 131; Mrs. Betty Wiseman, 132; The remaining 96 illustrations are from the Nancy Tonkin collection.

Introduction

Our definition of Beckenham is the former parish which survived as a distinct administrative unit, with only minor boundary changes except for the addition of West Wickham in 1934, until its incorporation into Greater London in 1965.

Beckenham extends roughly from Stumps Hill on the Southend Road in the north to West Wickham in the south, and from a point close to Bromley South Station on the east to Crystal Palace Parade in the west. What we have to remember is that these boundaries were decided when the parish consisted of a tiny country village with its associated farmsteads. Looking at early maps, it is easy to see how the boundaries of the parish followed the edges of fields or the lines of rivers or streams. Three rivers cross the area—the Beck, the Chaffinch and the Pool.

Beckenham is not an obviously historic place. There are no timber-framed buildings, no ancient fortifications, and even the parish church is a relatively modern creation. Appearances can be misleading, and this is particularly so in the case of Beckenham which has a long and fascinating history going back to at least the Roman occupation.

This is not a comprehensive account, for that would be impossible in the space available. What we have tried to do is to give an up-to-date outline, to indicate the factors which have moulded Beckenham into the place it is today and, by careful choice of examples and illustrations, to make the story come alive.

The circumstances by which Beckenham possesses a tongue of land, stretching up Crystal Palace Park Road and comprising part of Penge, and much of the Crystal Palace grounds, are strange. Borrowman, in his book *Beckenham Past and Present,* tells of a tradition that centuries ago an unknown corpse was found on the top of the hill where the Crystal Palace was built, and that, as the authorities of the parish in which it was found declined to bury it, those of Beckenham did so, claiming in return the land on either side of the body and a strip back to the original boundary of Beckenham parish. It is more likely that this was land which belonged to nearby Kent House, which at one time had grazing rights on Penge Common.

1. One of the 1868 cast-iron parish boundary posts which has survived in Summerhill Wood in Beckenham Place Park.

2. The roads and major buildings of pre-1850 Beckenham and the route of the Roman road.

Chapter I

The Past

Beckenham Village and Parish

The earliest known inhabitants of what is now Beckenham are believed to have arrived from the continent during the Iron Age, some two thousand years ago. Traces of their fortified encampment surrounded by ancient forest are, surprisingly, still to be seen at the highest part of the parish near Tootswood Road. The Saxon term 'Toot' denotes a look-out, or beacon point. 'Tootswood' may have been the site of an outpost of the Iron Age fort at Keston. This point was used in June 1887 for one of the great chain of bonfires, lit throughout the country, to commemorate Queen Victoria's Golden Jubilee. Due to the generosity of two local ladies, the Misses A. J. and W. S. Jay of 41 South Hill Road, the site has, since 1962, been in the care of the local authority with the proviso that it is never developed. In 1885 traces of Roman pottery were found there. The original occupiers of this camp were displaced or subdued by the Roman occupation of Britain in A.D.43. Whether any Roman or Romano-British buildings were erected in the area is purely a matter of conjecture since no significant remains have been uncovered. A Roman road leading from London to the iron workings near Lewes was constructed through the area, so it is quite possible that Roman buildings once existed and that their remains have been destroyed by later development. What happened when the Romans departed about A.D. 410 is not known, but Dr. Moore's pollen analysis at the Tootswood site suggests that an Anglo-Saxon settlement existed in the area round about the sixth century. This was possibly under the leadership of Beohha, the man from whom Beckenham is generally believed to derive its name. The district was well wooded, with open spaces where small communities existed by farming, hunting wild boar or deer, and by fishing in the local streams.

At the time of the Norman conquest Beckenham formed part of the possessions of Odo, Bishop of Bayeux and half brother of the King. It was well settled with both a manor and a mill as is recorded in Domesday Book. Nothing is known about the site of the mill but, as the basic geography of the area has not changed over the last thousand years, it is most likely to have been sited on the Beck near the present waterfall in Kelsey Park.

In the reign of Edward I the manor was owned by the de la Rochelles, who came originally from France. It later passed to the Bruyns when Sir Maurice Bruyn married Matilda Rokele.

.P . II . folins fe defd . Tra . ē . VIII . car . In dnĩo funt . II . 7 XXII.
uilli cū . VIII . bord hñt . VIII . car 7 dimid . Ibi . XII . ac̃ pti.
7 IIII . ferui . 7 uñ mold . 7 filua . LX . porc. ⌠ de rege . E.
T.R.E. 7 poft: ualeb . IX . lib . Modo: XIII . lib . Anfchil tenuit

In BROMLEY Hundred
Ansgot of Rochester holds BECKENHAM from the Bishop.
It answers for 2 sulungs. Land for 8 ploughs. In lordship 2.
   22 villagers with 8 smallholders have 8½ ploughs
   Meadow, 12 acres; 4 slaves; a mill; woodland, 60 pigs.
Value before 1066 and later £9; now £13.
   Askell held it from King Edward.

3. The entry in Domesday Book describing Beckenham with an English translation.

Elizabeth Bruyn, a great- great-granddaughter of this marriage, took William Brandon as her second husband, so that in the reign of Henry VII the manor passed to the Brandons. William Brandon was a standard-bearer at the battle of Bosworth Field, where he was slain. It is said that his son, Charles, Duke of Suffolk entertained Henry VIII on a journey to Hever to visit Anne Boleyn. The manor came into the hands of Sir Oliver St John and remained with the St Johns, afterwards Viscounts Bolingbroke, until late in the 18th century. It was sold to John Cator in 1773. The site of the manor house is almost certainly where the public hall and adjoining office building now stand in Bromley Road. Examination of the excavations for the foundations of the latter building in 1991 by one of the authors (ERI) revealed traces of a previous building, but the only artefacts recovered were a trade token and a wine vessel dating from the 16th century.

4. This photograph of the Old Manor House, taken in the 1870s, shows a basically Georgian-style building with a lower annexe attached to its northern end. From a report in the *Beckenham Journal* we know this attachment was older than the main structure. It was demolished when the council purchased the Manor House in 1882 for use as offices.

5. Foxgrove Farm, *c.*1870. The house was demolished about 1830 and this farmhouse erected in its place. This in turn was pulled down about 1878 and the remainder of its moat filled in to allow the estate to be developed for housing.

6. Kelsey Manor, *c*.1900. This mansion dates back to the 15th century but had been much enlarged and altered by the time this picture was taken. The last residents were the Hoare family, of banking fame, who provided the town with its first fire station and hospital.

7. The Mansion at Park Langley, *c*.1910. It was Sir Oliver Style of Langley who nearly doubled the size of the old parish church by adding north and south transepts, with family vaults underneath, during 1619-21.

Further substantial houses were constructed in the parish during the 15th-18th centuries, such as at Foxgrove, Elmers End, Langley and Kelsey. The Elmers End site was occupied during the 13th-15th centuries and was at one time owned by Robert de Retford, one of the king's itinerant judges. Thomas Motley's estate map of 1736 shows the unusual arrangement of two concentric moats but not the house. The area was bought in the 1860s by the Croydon Board of Health and the moated part levelled. It was later used as a sewage farm until the 1960s. Since then a large lake has been created and the site has been turned into a conservation area and bird sanctuary. Although now largely controlled by the Croydon Borough, it is partly in Beckenham with an entrance to it from Elmers End Road opposite Dorset Road.

Foxgrove was also moated and appears to have fared somewhat better than Elmers End. In the reign of Edward III, this manor belonged to John de Foxgrave. It seems to have changed hands quite frequently either by sale or by marriage until in the 18th century it had become part of the Langley estates, coming into the possession of Sir William Burrell in 1789. He sold it to his nephew Sir Peter Burrell IV, later Lord Gwydir. Four years later, by special Act of Parliament, it passed to the Cator family as part of a land-holding rationalisation.

The history of Kelsey and Langley is very different. The Kelsey mansion was built by William Brograve in the latter half of the 15th century. The Brograves resided there until towards the end of the 17th century when Peter Burrell, the first of that family to settle in the area, bought it in 1684.

Langley Place was a large farmstead owned (from the 13th-15th centuries) by the Longele family. During this time the Malmain family and the Violetts lived there for a period. At the beginning of the 16th century John Style, a London merchant, purchased the property and developed it into a gentleman's seat.

On the death of Sir Humphrey Style in 1718, his daughter, Dame Elizabeth Elwill, inherited the estate. A few years later her son, Sir Edmund Elwill, sold it to Hugh Raymond, a director of the South Sea Company. On his death in 1737 the property was inherited by his son Jones Raymond. His sister, Amy, married the second Peter Burrell of Kelsey and, on the death of her brother Jones in 1768, she succeeded to the Langley estates, as well as the Foxgrove Manor. Thus the Burrells owned Langley, Kelsey and Foxgrove. On Amy's death in 1789 this vast property of over 3,000 acres went to her grandson, Peter Burrell IV, and when he died in 1820 the connection of the Burrell family with Beckenham came to an end and the properties were put up for auction. The three-day sale at Garraway's Coffee House in October 1820 included Langley Farm, Langley Lodge, Kelsey Park, Eden Farm, Stone Farm, *The Three Tuns*, Elmer Lodge and many houses and some shops in the village. Langley was purchased by the Goodhart family whilst Kelsey was bought by Edward Grosse Smith, who in 1835 sold it on to the Hoares, the banking family. Both ceased to be family homes by the turn of the century.

Eden Farm was described as 'an elegant seat', the residence of William Eden who later became Lord Auckland. He entertained Pitt the Younger, Dundas, the elder Wilberforce, Vansittart, Lord Teignmouth, and other leaders of the Evangelical laity. His sister was married to Archbishop Moore of Canterbury. Eden Farm was large and easily able to accommodate the frequent overnight visitors who often totalled a dozen or more at a time. It was surrounded by superb gardens and shrubberies, with many large oak and elm trees in the grounds. The estate was open parkland covering an area almost down to Elmers End and Croydon Road. The mansion was a large white building in the classical style and stood where Crease Park is in Village Way. William Eden, 1st Lord Auckland, became Ambassador to Spain in 1787 and to the Netherlands two years later. He bought Eden Farm in 1807 but died seven years later. He was succeeded by his eldest son George, who later became Governor General of India.

Kent House, the first house in Kent on the route out of London, stood in Kent House Road not far from its junction with Lennard Road. It was an estate in the 12th century owned by a Norman nobleman. His grandson sold it to Sir Richard de la Rochelle, c.1246, who leased half of its value of quit rents to the hospital of St Katharine by the Tower of London. At the beginning of the 19th century it was used as a farm by James Randall and became known as Kent House Farm. The *Morning Post* in 1815 advertised the property as having common rights on Penge Common (*see* page 1). It continued as a farm until the turn of the century when it became first a nursing home and later a private hotel, before being demolished in 1957.

There were several other farms and lodges in the district during the 18th and 19th centuries but we have only touched on major large establishments. Farms towards the west side of the village were Elm Farm near the railway bridge in Barnmead Road and Thayers Farm nearer to Clock House station. Copers Cope Farm, off the Southend Road, was approximately 250

8. Kent House, *c*.1890. In the 17th century the Lethieulliers occupied the house and later it passed to John Julius Angerstein. Thackeray certainly stayed there and it is believed that Samuel Pepys, who was a friend of the Lethieullier family, may well have visited the house.

9. Stone Farm, seen here *c*.1910 only disappeared when the parade of shops was built in Wickham Road between the wars. Before the area became known as the 'Chinese Garage' it was called 'Looking Glass Corner'.

acres in extent and stretched to the New Beckenham area with footpaths to Kent House Farm. The farmhouse on the corner of Copers Cope Road still stands today, and is a listed building. Stone Farm was at the top of what is now Stone Park Avenue near the Chinese Garage. These farms supplied the area with milk and meat—the cows being milked and the cattle slaughtered on the premises.

Of the more modest buildings of old Beckenham, *The George Inn*, said to be over 300 years old, is the only property in the High Street to survive to the present day. The petty sessions were once held there. Three other buildings existed long enough to be recorded by the camera. The Old Wood House, a timber-framed building of primitive basic construction, stood where W. H. Smith's now stands and was demolished in the 1930s; Gordon House, on whose site Sainsbury's was opened in 1915; and the Manor House with its covered entrance way.

Austin's pork butchers, next to *The Three Tuns* public house, was originally a gardener's cottage and said to date from at least the 17th century. It was not demolished until the 1960s, after having been in the Austin family for over one hundred years. Elm Cottage, which stood on the corner of what is now Village Way, was demolished in 1914 to make way for Beckenham's first cinema, The Pavilion, and may also have been a simple timber-framed building. It was here that Borrowman, the historian was born.

10. Old Wood House in the High Street, *c*.1905. This picturesque old building may have been built as a yeoman's hall. When it was demolished it was discovered that it had originally been one large hall with a central fireplace and only a hole in the roof to let out the smoke.

11. The exact age of *The George Inn* is not known but a Richard King is recorded as paying hearth tax there in 1662. The covered entrance way to the Manor House can be seen on the left of the picture.

12. Austin's shop by the side of *The Three Tuns* public house, *c.*1900. The lower part was of brick and stucco, and the upper part of green oak weatherboarding on timber-framing. The plaster was made of straw and cow-dung.

13. Shortlands Farmhouse, *c*.1918. This old building is reputed to have been the model for the cottage in Enid Blyton's Noddy stories.

Other old buildings still standing today are the cottage near The Chinese Garage, the Bailiff's Cottage in Manor Way, Langley Chapel, and the farmhouse on the corner of Shortlands and Bromley Roads.

Beckenham, unlike nearby Bromley, is not on a main road to the coast and this, together with its position, an easy ride to and from the capital, probably contributed to its growing popularity among rich London merchants as a site for a country home. The number of memorials to wealthy gentry and their servants formerly to be found in and around the parish church is one indication of this. Several references in the church records show that many of the gentry had black or coloured servants at this time. In 1715 a twice-weekly coach service from Beckenham to London is a sign that there was sufficient custom from within the parish.

The mid-17th-century hearth and poll tax returns for the parish of Beckenham have survived and when these are compared with the first national census taken 200 years later it can be seen that there had been a very substantial increase in population, including many wealthy people. The poll tax return contains the names of 203 people so, if we assume an equal number of children and that some of the inhabitants managed to escape the collectors, the population of the parish in 1645 must have been round about five hundred.

The interesting feature of this list, apart from the disparity of rate between that of the gentry (£10-£30) and that for the parson (1s.) and ordinary folk including wives of any status (6d.), is that it reveals only four households of any size and that even these, including Langley, had very few servants. None of the substantial houses, which we know existed at the end of the 18th century, feature in the return. There were probably less than 100 houses in the village at that time.

This situation is confirmed by the hearth tax return made only some 20 years later. In all, 52 persons were charged for 181 hearths, and 40 were non-chargeable as they did not possess more than one. Hearths were difficult to conceal, so the information given here is likely to be more accurate than that in the previous poll tax return. Once again a picture of a parish with relatively few, very modest houses appears. Only four dwellings have more hearths than the seven of *The George Inn*, the only building surviving to the present day and which can now be seen to be fairly small. The 24-hearth dwelling occupied by John Scott is obviously Langley, the next with 12 hearths occupied by a Mr. Brograve is Kelsey whilst the other two, each with nine, are assumed to be the Old Manor House and either Foxgrove or the Rectory.

The Beckenham Old Manor House has already been referred to but just across the road, in 1789, the Rev. William Rose built his new rectory. The design of the garden with its vista across open pasture is interesting for it seems to have been copied from, or inspired by, that of the Manor House, where the middle ground was occupied by lawns and a lake, or possibly of Village Place or Beckenham Lodge. Village Place, we know, was rebuilt in 1717 and its extensive grounds stretched the full length of the back of the properties on the north side of the High Street. The Beck had obviously been diverted and landscaped to accommodate the gardens of Gordon House and the other Manor House and it is interesting to speculate whether this would have been allowed unless they were already in existence when the Village Place garden was laid out.

Development was not confined to the village itself. Clock House, Shortlands House, The Hall and Beckenham Place, all belong to this period.

Clock House was built early in the 18th century and Sir Piercy Brett, 'Admiral of the Blue', lived there until his death in 1781. The substantial, redbrick mansion was built close to the main road from Penge to Beckenham and later the nearby railway station was to take its name from the house. At the beginning of the last century John Cator's brother, Joseph, lived there with his large family—he had six sons and several daughters—until his death, after which it had various tenants. The house was demolished in 1896 but the stables stayed as part of Horsman's Nursery until they were finally pulled down in 1926.

Shortlands House was built at the start of the 18th century. It was here that George Grote, the historian, was born in 1794. For many years he was an M.P. and introduced the 1833 Ballot

14. Presumably wishing to be one up on his prosperous new neighbours, William Rose hired the Adam brothers in 1875, to design his new rectory (situated on what is now Church Avenue). Two years previously, he had invited the famous landscape architect, Humphry Repton, to advise him on the layout of the garden.

15. The Clock House, c.1895. The well wooded gardens contained a sizeable lake with ornamental fountain, and the extensive stable block was surmounted by a large clock which gave the building its name. The stable clock was removed and taken to Beckenham Place where it can still be seen today.

Bill. George Grote was offered a peerage which he refused, but on his death in 1871 he was buried in Westminster Abbey. Later Shortlands House became the residence of W. A. Wilkinson, an M.P., whose family was largely responsible for the building of St Mary's church. The grounds of the house covered over 130 acres, much of which was sold as building plots in 1863. At the auction the land realised nearly £500 per acre, an incredibly high sum for those days. Earlier this century the house ceased to be used as a private residence and became an hotel until 1949, when it was purchased by the Roman Catholic diocese for use as a preparatory school.

By far the most influential of the 18th-century newcomers were the Cators. John Cator (1728-1806) purchased the Lordship of the Manor of Beckenham in 1773, added first Copers Cope Farm, then Foxgrove Farm and finally Kent House Farm, thus rapidly building up a very large estate of properties both inside and outside the parish. Shortly after he bought the Old Manor House in 1773 he decided to build Beckenham Place further north, diverting the main road in the process so that it did not pass too close to his new mansion. Situated at the top of Stumps Hill it commanded a fine view over Kent and London. On John Cator's death Beckenham Place was leased to William Peters who formed a private cricket ground there in 1835. The mansion was later used as a boys' school, then a sanatorium, before becoming the Golf Club House when the L.C.C. purchased Beckenham Place in 1928.

John Cator was a wealthy timber merchant who lived the life of the rich country landowner. His wife, Mary, was the daughter of the distinguished botanist, Peter Collinson F.R.S., and the couple entertained a succession of famous people including the celebrated Dr. Johnson, who is on record as describing Beckenham Place as one of the finest places at which he was ever a guest. He was a frequent visitor and formed the library and catalogued it. The library is now in Woodbastwick Hall, in Norfolk, the seat of the Cators. Mrs. Thrale, Fanny Burney, Sir Joshua Reynolds, and the Adams brothers all came to Beckenham Place. There seems little doubt that John Cator corresponded with the Swedish botanist Linnaeus, but it is unlikely that the latter ever visited the house or, as Borrowman relates, planted trees and shrubs in the grounds.

16. John Cator belonged to the second generation of the family to live in the area, his father (also named John), having moved to Bromley in the early part of the century. The main family residence was Beckenham Place with two subsidiary houses, Clock House on Penge (now Beckenham) Road and The Hall on Bromley Road.

17. Beckenham Place, *c.*1890. In 1784 John Cator added the ornamental frontage which had formerly belonged to Wricklemarsh Park at Blackheath. Over the door was the Cator family motto, 'Nihil sine Labore'.

Chapter II
The Creation of Beckenham Town

The Building and Growth of the various Estates

The first survey of 1798-99 and Pigot's 1839 *Directory of Kent* provide us with the first really detailed picture of the village of Beckenham. It straggled along the main road from what we now call Thornton's Corner to the junction with the roads to Croydon and Penge, separated from the tiny hamlet of Elmers End by open country. The Rector and the Lord of the Manor lived up the hill outside the village proper. There were no road or street names as we know them now; all the early directories simply give an address as 'the village'. Pigot tells us there were 35 tradesmen and that the nobility and gentry numbered eighteen. Thirteen years later, just before the opening of the Crystal Palace, the gentry had almost doubled to 33 and were served by 44 tradesmen. Beckenham even at this time was a fast growing, high-class community. This was to be dwarfed by the changes which took place soon afterwards when proximity to London and the arrival of the railways led to the development of the area. This was to be of great financial benefit to the Cator family.

John Cator (1728-1806) and his wife Mary built Beckenham Place in the late 1770s. They only had one child, Maria, who died at the age of three. As a result, in 1806 the estate passed to John's nephew, John Barwell Cator, the eldest of the numerous children of his brother Joseph who lived at Clock House. Barwell Cator was a very different man from his uncle. Eccentric in his later years and a keen sportsman, he spent much of his time in Ireland, the birthplace of his wife, Elizabeth. In 1813 he purchased Woodbastwick Hall in Norfolk, the better to pursue his sporting interests, leaving Beckenham Place to be occupied by a series of tenants. Being close to London, the development of Beckenham was inevitable but it was Barwell Cator's gambling debts which sparked off the family need to convert land into cash. In 1825 he obtained parliamentary approval to develop his estates for housing. At one time he mortgaged many of the freeholds of his properties to the Prudential Assurance Company for £187,000, a truly vast sum in the middle of the 19th century.

The most important member of the Cator family concerned with Beckenham was Peter, the youngest son of Joseph, who returned from a career in the Indian civil service just in time to save the family fortunes. He persuaded his brother to hand over control of the Beckenham estate to his eldest son Albemarle, and to appoint himself as agent. Peter, unlike his brother John Barwell Cator, seems to have inherited his uncle's shrewdness and business sense. He lived on the estate at The Hall and took an active interest in the affairs of the parish. He sold land in 1854 for a railway on nominal terms providing trains did not run on Sundays during the time of divine service, and for housing which had to conform to strict up-market standards, with plenty of accommodation for servants, carriages and gardens. Many of these large houses have now been replaced by blocks of flats or even by small estates of town houses.

The first houses on the estate were large and detached, and had a minimum of half an acre of ground. This was later reduced to one third of an acre when the sale of the houses slowed down. The roads on the Cator Estate were unmade and owners of the properties had to pay a fair share of the expense of maintaining and keeping in good and substantial repair the roads, footpaths and water drains. They were charged according to the footage of the road frontages of the houses. These regulations also covered walls and fences surrounding the property. Most of the houses were built with stabling and coach houses.

A conveyance for a house in Albemarle Road contains the following stipulation:

> No part of the land or any building erected, or to be erected thereon shall at any time be used for the purpose of the business or occupation of a Schoolmaster, Schoolmistress, Boarding Housekeeper, Auctioneer, or Estate Agent or any art or Mystery or of any trade business or manufacture whatsoever nor shall any notice or inscription board plate or placard relating to the same or any of them to be placed in or upon or about the premises and no building erected or to be erected as aforesaid shall at any time be used for any other purpose than that of a private residence.

It is no wonder that the Cator Estate was at one time considered to be the stockbroker belt of South London. However, things did change because, before the turn of the century, some of the large houses were being used as private schools and, before the First World War, a house in Beckenham Park was being used as a hospital or nursing home for alcoholics.

At first the houses were not numbered but named instead. This must have become a nightmare for the postman, especially as the names were often changed when there was a new owner. One house in Albemarle Road was called 'Rolandseck' in a document dated 1894. Later it changed to 'Exford' but by 1901 it had become 'Heatherdene'. It was finally numbered 83. The property had been leasehold but the freehold was bought in 1963 when it changed hands once more.

Between 1860-90, however, a completely new Victorian town was to rise on what had been fields and gardens, and the town became centred on the vicinity of the station. This and later developments are reflected in the rapid growth in population, something which was to continue, apart from the war years, almost to the present time.

We are fortunate that the Ordnance Survey made a detailed large-scale study of the area in 1861. So it is not only convenient but also quite legitimate to take 1857, the date of the opening of the station, as the starting point for the transformation of Beckenham from a village into a town.

Year	Population	Inhabited Dwellings	Uninhabited Dwellings	Dwgs under construction
1801	955	159	-	-
1811	1,093	164	-	-
1821	1,180	196	-	-
1831	1,288	238	-	-
1841	1,608	285	-	-
1851	1,688	307	13	2
1861	2,124	362	10	7
1871	6,090	976	123	66
1881	13,045	1,995	175	79
1891	20,707	3,451	183	55
1901	26,331	4,701	308	166
1911	31,692	6,227	612	53
1921	33,345	6,925	267	158
1931	43,832	10,308	311	-
1941	51,000*	16,431	518#	-
1951	54,116	19,250*	348#	-
1961	56,139	20,000*	-	-

Notes: The figures for 1801 to 1931 refer to Beckenham Parish, Local Board Area and U.D.C. Area; for 1941 to 1961 they refer to the Borough of Beckenham excluding West Wickham. * - estimates. # - including West Wickham.

Sources: Census returns, Council Minutes & Housing Surveys.

18. The population of Beckenham. This table, taken from an unpublished book entitled *The Railways of Beckenham* by Andrew Hajducki, illustrates the rapid growth of the town once the station opened.

19. The *Station Hotel, c.*1905. The earliest detailed Ordnance Survey in 1861 shows building well under way on the Cator Estate and this hotel, surrounded by orchards and gardens, standing roughly where Beckenham Green is now. The hounds last met there in 1905.

20. Beckenham Grove, *c.*1915. Many of the large houses in the Beckenham and Shortlands areas were used to billet soldiers during the First World War.

Gloucester Terrace, a row of 13 houses behind the National School, had a well to provide the water supply. It was in one of these houses that the Cator Estates had their office until they later moved to a gatehouse of Beckenham Place. The early provision of these working-class houses illustrates that Peter Cator was well aware of the need to provide a variety of housing on his estate.

Shortlands was the other part of the parish which was developed at the same time and in a similar manner to the Cator estates. Here the dominant landowner was W. A. Wilkinson, who lived at Shortlands House from 1848 until his death in 1865. The name Shortlands may be derived from the medieval description of the size of strips of land which had been divided into cornfields or ploughed pasturage.

Until the arrival of the railway in 1858 Shortlands, which lies mainly in the Ravensbourne valley, was known as 'a gentleman's seat, with picturesque surroundings, a farmstead and a few neat cottages'. A little later *The Bromley Record* noted that the large Victorian detached houses set amongst mature trees transformed the estate into a fashionable neighbourhood. The houses in Tootswood Road and Durham Avenue were built around 1890 and further developments took place after the First World War.

The pattern of roads was decided at a fairly early stage and was usually adhered to. The 1864 Cator Estate plan printed on the endpapers of this book demonstrates this well. Mote Road was renamed The Avenue, presumably when Foxgrove Farm was demolished, and the remains of the moat filled in. The same situation applied on the Wilkinson development at Shortlands where the roads were laid out and a church was built at a very early stage.

21. Ravensbourne Avenue, *c.*1900. The road through Summer Hill Wood was never constructed as originally planned, being replaced by Downs Hill, Crab Hill and Ravensbourne Avenue as a consequence of the Catford Loop Line railway development in the early 1890s.

22. The Avenue, *c*.1900. A wide, straight, tree-lined road running from Beckenham Junction through towards Shortlands, typical of the Cator Estate.

23. Shortlands Estate advertising map, *c*.1870. Most of the properties and roads illustrated can be identified today. Note, however, that the water works has been left out and the route to Beckenham is made to look like a Scottish glen, presumably to improve the sales appeal!

24. Burrell Row. It is probable that the distinctive terraced properties of Burrell Row and Manor View belong to the early 1870s, providing much needed accommodation for the rapidly growing population of workers in the new shops and service trades.

Whilst the Cator and Wilkinson estates were being developed, equally rapid construction was going on in the town itself on land owned by the Cators, the Hoares at Kelsey, the Lea Wilsons of Village Place and by the Church. Rectory Road was constructed in the very early 1870s. Leases for the properties on Lea Wilson land in Lea Road, Burnhill Road and Stanmore Terrace also date from 1873 and that of Thornton's Corner a year later.

By the beginning of the 1880s the new centre of Beckenham next to the parish church was fully developed. This area was almost totally destroyed during the Second World War and the little Church Road was to disappear completely.

In 1866 the Duke of Westminster sold Porcupine Field in Beckenham, close to Penge East station, on very favourable terms to the 'Metropolitan Association for Improving the Dwellings of the Industrious Classes'. On this land the charity erected its only country estate and named it Alexandra after the Princess of Wales. The four roads were named Albert, Edward, Victor, and Princess (later changed to Princes).

The Birkbeck Estate was begun in the 1870s when land was bought by the Birkbeck Freehold Land Society. It was not fully developed until just before the First World War when Allen Road was built. The Churchfields Road area had belonged to the Beckenham Parish Church Council. This is why Seward and Clement Roads are the only two roads having direct links between Churchfields and Blandford Roads, as they were built on the only plot of land owned by the Birkbeck Estate. It also accounts for the reason why Sultan Street and Blandford Avenue are cul-de-sacs and Kimberley Road is a crescent.

If the Cator and Wilkinson estates were to provide the earliest high-class housing developments in Beckenham, they were to be followed later by one even more ambitious. In 1908 the firm of H. & G. Taylor purchased the bulk of the Langley Estate, including the mansion, from the trustees of the Goodhart Estate. The estate they planned was to be self-contained with its own shopping centre, post office, community hall, tennis courts and golf course.

25. The High Street, *c*.1903. Note the Royal Coat of Arms over the first shop on the left. This was Hagger's the butchers.

26. This end of Albemarle Road, *c*.1905, was very busy with its shops and the main post office.

27. Albert Road, seen here *c*.1910, was unusual as the houses were semi-detached and each had a garden, at a time when most Victorian working-class houses were terraces or tenements.

28. Birkbeck Road, *c*.1909. There was a footbridge across the railway between the two parts of the Birkbeck Estate and before the Second World War was closed one day a year to indicate that it was railway and not public property.

29. Wickham Way, c.1925. The houses were all to be architecturally designed in a variety of sizes and styles with none exactly alike. Each was to have a substantial garden and to be approached from tree and shrub lined roads to partially conceal them from the gaze of casual passers by. Even the lamp posts were specially designed for the Estate.

30. Coldman House, c.1920. Unlike the Victorian and Edwardian houses of the Cator and Wilkinson Estates, Taylor's houses looked surprisingly modern and, apart from the size of the gardens and absence of garages, would not look out of place on a present-day, up-market development. Noticeable too for the Edwardian period is the lack of staff accommodation.

The cost of these magnificent homes seems almost unbelievable today. In an example quoted in the sales brochure, a house costing £850 is purchased by paying £200 down, borrowing the remainder from an Assurance Co. and repaying this over 20 years in half yearly instalments totalling £56 2s. 4d. per annum. Whitecroft Way was one of the first roads on the new estate. It was named after Richard de Wytecroft who lived in the 13th century and was connected with Langley. There had been a road there for some centuries running from Langley to Foxgrove. One of the first houses to be erected in Whitecroft Way won an award at the 1912 Ideal Homes Exhibition.

Apart from laying out the roads, many of which were named after historic persons connected with the estate on the recommendation of Robert Borrowman, the first development was the golf club. A club house had been built onto the old mansion, which had required substantial renovation after lying empty since 1903 when it was vacated by the Goodharts. Sadly both were destroyed by fire in 1913 and replaced by the present club house. The club was opened by its newly elected president, Mr. H. W. Forster M.P., on 28 May 1910. Tennis followed soon after and nine courts were laid down by 1911.

Unlike the sporting facilities, the other planned amenities were never provided. This is a pity, for the shopping centre, planned for what is now the junction of Styles and Whitecroft Way, was a truly remarkable proposal for the time. It was to consist of a circle of shops with flats over the top and a covered winter garden with bandstand, palms and statuary in the centre. The development attracted a lot of attention and seems to have made steady progress, though whether the plan for a motor bus service, which it was claimed would meet the principal trains at Beckenham Junction, was ever carried out is not certain. The outbreak of war stopped the building completely. Much of the postwar development was carried out by others and at a somewhat lower standard.

The Taylors seemed to have had a flair for publicity and, when in 1929 they opened a garage at Looking Glass Corner at the entrance to the estate, it was built in Eastern style, and ever since it has been known as the Chinese Garage. The design is something of a mystery. The theory that it owes its design to a local landowner with an interest in things oriental seems unlikely, for Langley Court was already owned by Wellcome and the remainder of the Goodhart Estate was controlled by Taylors themselves. The suggestion that the inspiration arose from a competition run by the *Daily Express* to find the most original filling station, and in which it won a prize, seems the more likely explanation.

There was a reference to Elmers End in an indenture dated 1682 relating to 'house, buildings, grounds and land known as 'Eastfield' situated at Elmers End, occupied by Stephen Randell and Thomas Fanster'. Another early reference was in 1775 when mention was made of the great need for small houses for the 'industrious shepherds and labourers of the Parish'. It was decided to ask John Cator, the Lord of the Manor, to build 12 houses—four of which were possibly those put up near to the *William IV* at Elmers End Green and another four near to *The Rising Sun*. These latter ones were demolished in 1962 to make way for new council flats.

It was not until much later that Elmers End was really developed. Besides the cottages at the *William IV* there was a parade of shops on the other side of Croydon Road, with a few quite large houses in Langley Road. The district came into its own with the building of the council estate in Goddard and Adams Roads and Shirley Crescent between 1920 and 1930. At the same time housing developments were started in the Eden Park area. By the early 1930s most of the available land had been covered, with the exception of the playing fields in Stanhope Grove, Balmoral Avenue, and the back of Marian Vian School.

31. Elmers End shops, *c.*1907. This parade of shops is between Langley Road and Goddard Road. The *William IV* public house can be seen at the end of the road on the left.

32. Langley Road, Elmers End, *c.*1910. Houses did not go the full length of Goddard Road until a few council houses were built at the top end in the 1920s.

33. Upper Elmers End Road, *c.*1925. With the building of the council estate Elmers End changed more than most in the parish.

34. Eden Way was built in 1936 almost on the boundary of the borough.

35. Elmers End, seen here early this century, was virtually all farm land and woods, a very rural part of Beckenham. It remained largely undeveloped until after the First World War.

36. An early view of the Davis Estate. The Drive was originally intended to be called Wilson Avenue, but the proposal was overruled by the council.

At the end of the First World War there was still a lot of open country in the parish and working farms could be found within walking distance of the High Street. Even the centre of the town was taken up by gardens and meadows belonging either to the Lea Wilsons or the church. By 1939 most of this land had been built on and the town had become in fact, if not in name, part of London. Village Place was demolished in the early 1920s and its grounds together with those of the rectory replaced by the Davis Estate of small terrace houses selling for £950 and the new roads of The Drive, Church Avenue and The Crescent.

This rapid development of the southern part and centre of the town at a much higher density than the older Cator, Wilkinson and Taylor Estates resulted in the return of the commercial centre of the commercial town to its original position along the lower High Street. This was assisted by the council who had compulsorily purchased land along almost its entire length so that it could be widened. It also resulted in the replacement of old shops by more modern properties which were taken up by firms such as Montague Burton, W. H. Smith, and Woolworths.

Chapter III

Beckenham Town

Administration and Services

Until 1872 the only authority dealing with local affairs within the parish was the vestry, a committee of local landowners and gentry chaired by the rector. The records of Beckenham vestry have survived from 1774 as have a few isolated ones dating back to the 1680s. The vestry was a versatile body which dealt with both public and church matters, many of which are still relevant today. In 1778 we read that it conducted a survey on the willingness of the inhabitants to be inoculated against smallpox at the parish expense. A few years later Sunday observance was a hot subject. The vestry decided that no shop should sell any goods after ten in the morning nor should any individual shave or dress their hair after the same hour. Anyone found offending was liable to be placed in the 'cage' and left to ponder the inscription over the door; Live and Repent.

In 1869 the vestry passed a resolution that 'as it was difficult to keep the old and thickly filled church-yard in order by hand the church-wardens at St George's church should be authorised to admit sheep for the purpose'.

The construction of the London to Croydon canal, which passed through the north-west corner of the parish, and its replacement in 1839 by a railway led to an influx of navvies. It was, however, the construction of the Crystal Palace in 1852-54, a considerable part of the grounds of which was in Beckenham, that had the most far-reaching effect. At that time scant regard was paid to parish or even county boundaries for the financial and planning implications were minimal.

37. Disorderly and inebriated persons would be put in the Cage until they sobered up. It was at the bottom of Church Hill before being removed in November 1856.

PLAN OF THE GARDENS AND PARK

from Norwood.

from Croydon

to Dulwich

to Upper Sydenham

DULWICH WOOD

CRYSTAL PALACE

UPPER RESERVOIR

A

C

B   B

INTERMEDIATE RESERVOIR

GRAND FOUNTAIN   GRAND FOUNTAIN

to Sydenham

LAKE AND EXTINCT ANIMALS

CRICKET GROUND

RAILWAY

ARCHERY C°

BECKENHAM BOUNDARY

38. The Crystal Palace grounds, seen here around 1860, straddled the Kent-Surrey boundary and involved no less than three parishes of Battersea, Dulwich and Beckenham. During its construction the streets of the once peaceful village resounded to the boots of 200 navvies who lodged in Beckenham and walked the two miles each way, to and from work.

39. The old fire and police stations. When 7 Kelsey Square was being re-decorated in 1961, a painted panel was discovered under the layers of wallpaper in the passageway, giving details of the offices and officers of the board.

Once completed, the enormous glasshouse, ablaze with light in the evenings and replete with every modern development, was visible from almost every part of the parish, a constant reminder of the technical changes taking place in the world outside. As a result of the opening of the palace, land in the north-west part of the parish became much in demand for building large houses, with mains water provided by the Lambeth Water Co. and gas by the Crystal Palace and District Co. at Bell Green, Sydenham, luxuries not at first available in the rest of the parish.

The rapid development in housing, particularly in the part of the parish nearest to the Crystal Palace, compelled the vestry to introduce a measure of control over the activities of its residents and the disposal of their waste. A sanitary sub-committee had already been set up in 1848 to remove nuisances such as ill-sited pig-sties, and ten years later this became a Nuisances Removal Committee with increased powers granted under an 1855 Act of Parliament.

The 1872 Public Health Act divided the country into urban and rural sanitary districts whose authorities took over most of the duties formerly exercised by the parish vestry. Beckenham found itself in the Bromley Rural Sanitary District's area with its affairs administered by a parochial sub-committee. This was an affront to many of the inhabitants of the rapidly growing township and in 1878 it was authorised to elect a local board, able to appoint officers and to decide its own affairs independently of Bromley. This remained the case until 1894 when increased urbanisation led Kent County Council to replace the board with an urban district council.

The Beckenham Local Board established an office above the fire station building, which had been provided for that purpose by Peter Hoare of Kelsey, and later converted two of the adjacent dwelling houses in Kelsey Square into additional accommodation. This extra space was soon totally inadequate, so in 1882 the opportunity was taken to purchase the old Manor House and the immediately adjacent garden and outhouses for £5,075 including fittings. The older part of the Manor House was demolished and its site sold to a Public Hall Company set up for the purpose. The remaining building only required little adaptation. The stables were extended to house the fire brigade with accommodation for seven horses and a loft above for hay and fodder. A new front was added in 1884-85 to tone in with the adjoining new bank premises and sadly this is the only part of the building to survive until the present day.

L. & C. Bank, Council Offices, Public Hall & Fire Station, Beckenham.

40. Bromley Road with Bank and Old Manor House, *c*.1909. Much of the cost of the Old Manor House was recouped by selling off parts of the garden to the London & County Bank (now part of the National Westminster Bank) and to the Metropolitan Police.

41. Opening of the new Town Hall. On 20 October 1932 the building was declared open by H.R.H. Prince George, Duke of Kent. The school children who lined the route managed to cheer loudly in spite of the rain.

The town continued to grow rapidly as did the services required to be provided by the council. The Education Office moved to 14 Bromley Road; the Public Health Office to the building on the corner of Burnhill Road and the High Street; the Surveyor's Department to a shop on Church Hill, while the Electricity Showrooms, then part of the council's administration, were on the corner of Manor Road and Church Hill.

In 1926 the council purchased the old rectory and much of its garden to build a town hall large enough for all the council departments for the foreseeable future. The building was completed in 1932 with the help of a grant from the Government's unemployment relief scheme

In September 1935 the town was granted Municipal Borough status and the Lord Mayor of London arrived in his state coach to present the Charter of Incorporation to the mayor and council.

Beckenham's pride was to be shortlived. Between the wars every piece of open ground not dedicated as parkland was built on, and by 1939 housing estates had obscured the boundaries between the separate communities

42. The Town Hall, c.1935. Beckenham Council was able to organise its affairs much more efficiently once all departments were housed in one central building.

which had formerly made up the area. Urban facilities were now more appropriate than those designed for rural commmunities and it was for this reason that in 1934 West Wickham had become part of Beckenham Urban District. In 1965 the final blow fell; the town was transferred from the County of Kent to Greater London. Worse still, administration became centred in Bromley, and Beckenham became part of the London Borough of Bromley. The council buildings in which the town had taken so much pride gradually became redundant and were demolished, the old Council Hall in 1990 and the Town Hall in 1992.

So far we have concentrated on the development of local government in the town but services also grew in size and complexity and, just like administration, were gradually taken out of local hands.

Probably the first undertaking to be run by the local authority, apart from road maintenance, was the workhouse and it was also the first to pass into the hands of a larger authority, in this case the Bromley Union in 1836. It is not known when the workhouse opened but it was sited on the Bromley Road well away from the village itself. Its spartan conditions were described in some detail in Borrowman's *Beckenham, Past and Present*. There were 14 beds in all, so that, on those occasions when the house had over 24 inmates, it must have been very overcrowded. Lights were not allowed except in the hall, which was lit by three candlesticks.

The supply of towels for the whole establishment never exceeded eight, and ablutions were probably made under the pump in the yard. The supply of sheets for the 14 beds never exceeded 29, and there was only one pillow case! According to the inventories there was only one flannel gown, used no doubt for the invalids. It was neither attractive nor comfortable, and it was not uncommon for the inmates to run away. When caught they were put in the lock-up which was scantily furnished with a chaff bed and a blanket.

The police force was the first service to become London based. With the growth of population and crime, the village constable appointed by the vestry had become quite inappropriate. In 1833 Alderman Wilson who lived in Village Place applied for Beckenham to come under the jurisdiction of the Metropolitan Police and, when he became Lord Mayor of London six years later, his request was granted. A cottage next to *The Three Tuns* public house became the police station manned by a sergeant and seven constables. By 1865 this had become two sergeants and ten constables under the supervision of a mounted inspector based at Lewisham. The present police station on Church Hill was built on part of the Old Manor House garden purchased from the local board and was opened by Squire Lea Wilson on 1 June 1885. The old police station was demolished in 1936 to provide access for parking behind *The Three Tuns*.

The local gentry were not only concerned about crime but also the dangers of fire. Sir Francis Tress Barry of Clock House organised a volunteer brigade for which Peter Hoare adapted one of the buildings at the entrance to the Kelsey Estate for the engine. The brigade passed into the control of the local board and moved to a new station adapted from the Old Manor House stables in 1882. The original fire station remains to this day, little altered inside though now occupied by a greengrocer. Fires must have burnt fairly slowly in those days for not only had the local turncock to be roused to turn on the water, horses had also to be acquired

43. Fire practice at Foxgrove Farm, *c*.1875. Until 1886 Charles Purvis, the tenant of Foxgrove farm, was Hon. Superintendent and it was at the farm that the brigade did much of its practice.

44. Beckenham's 'First Aid Tri-Car' was purchased in 1908 at a cost of £122. It was designed to speed two firemen with basic equipment to a blaze to do what they could whilst the main engine was 'horsed up' and could come galloping to the scene!

to harness to the engine. At that time any passing vehicle could be stopped and its horse used for the fire engine. In July 1885 there was a fire in Southend Lane and the engine could not go because the horse was ill! The gallant firemen proceeded to the scene by cab. Apparently no-one thought to put the cab horse to the fire engine!

The large area covered by the parish and the slow speed of the appliances on the rough unmade roads necessitated sub-depots to cover areas such as Birkbeck, Lawrie Park and Shortlands. For example, in 1890 a hose-reel shed was erected in Valley Road next to the parish room and replaced in 1902 by a purpose-built engine house with accommodation in Station Road. This sub-station closed in 1913 when the brigade acquired its second motorised fire engine and was later demolished. The Birkbeck station was in Avenue Road and a third one in Alexandra Recreation Ground.

The Bromley Road fire station was extended and adapted over the years. It housed, at one time or another, a social club, a dentist, and the Saunders and Abbott motor dealers. In 1929 the council built houses for the firemen at the rear of the station and later, after the incorporation of West Wickham, a modern station was opened in Glebe Way. The war resulted in the demise of small local brigades with their limited resources and varying, often incompatible, equipment. All brigades were nationalised from 1941 to 1948 and after this the responsibility for firefighting in Beckenham passed first to Kent County Council and then, after the 1965 local government reorganisation, to the London Fire Brigade. As a result the West Wickham fire station was closed and the Bromley Road station replaced by a combined fire and ambulance station in Beckenham Road, which opened in 1986.

Even by the middle of the 19th century services in Beckenham were much simpler than today. Water was obtained from wells and pumps, and the waste from primitive privies ran into cesspools often sited in close proximity to the water supply. One of the village pumps has survived at the corner of Kelsey Square, but there once were several, including one standing in the middle of the road at the bottom of Church Hill. The first public sewer was constructed in 1860, and Borrowman recalls that a few years later Dr. Stilwell called the attention of the vestry to the impure water supply which existed in the village. The Shortlands pumping station came into use in the 1860s.

The building of the Crystal Palace, partly in the parish, meant that not only was the Beckenham parish vestry's permission required to introduce gas and water to the area but there was a strong and growing commercial incentive to do so. Thames water was supplied by the Lambeth Water Company from a reservoir near the Palace and many were the complaints about its quality and continuity until 1903, when all the private water companies in the London area were taken over by the newly constituted Metropolitan Water Board. Lambeth's water did not reach as far as Wilkinson's Shortlands estate, for which the water pumped from a well sunk in a meadow near the railway by the North Kent Water Company.

On 2 September 1854, the vestry gave the Crystal Palace & District Gas Co. permission to introduce gas into the parish at their expense and some time later three street lamps were erected, one at the junction of Penge (now Beckenham) and Croydon Roads, one in the vicinity of the Cage and Pound, and one near the rectory gate. There was no street lighting prior to this and, once the sun went down, the only light in even the grandest of homes came from candles or oil lamps. In 1864 street lighting was extended to include the whole length of the road from Penge to Beckenham Junction. *The George Inn* was one of the first buildings in Beckenham to be lit by gas.

45. Beckenham Cottage Hospital, *c*.1911. The hospital opened in 1872 through the generosity of Peter Hoare of Kelsey Manor, who provided both the land and building for a four-bed hospital at a nominal rent.

46. Stone Park Maternity Hospital. This replaced the Beckenham & Penge Maternity Home in 1939 and closed in 1986. The site is now a sheltered housing complex owned by Morden College.

Beckenham Cottage Hospital is yet another example of local initiative and generosity, providing a service which in its time was a source of great local pride only to decline later into the relative obscurity of a large regional authority. Patients were charged sixpence a day and the building also housed public baths and wash houses. Peter Hoare's death in 1877 resulted in a crisis, as the executors of his estate demanded a commercial rent. The value of the facility was so appreciated that donations not only enabled this rent to be paid but the freehold to be purchased in 1887. A year later, a four-room extension named after Squire Lea Wilson was added. An operating theatre was built, followed only two years later by a children's ward and a near doubling of the hospital's capacity to 31 beds. X-ray facilities were provided by Messrs. Muirhead of Elmers End in 1902.

The hospital passed into the hands of the state in 1948 but expansion continued almost to the present time when uncertainty as to its future role has cast a cloud over the scene. Beckenham's hospital facilities were not confined to the Cottage Hospital. Maternity services were provided at a house in Croydon Road from 1919 until 1939 when a purpose-built maternity hospital opened in Stone Park Avenue. This was closed in 1986 and the site sold to Morden College. In 1924 the world renowned Bethlem Hospital purchased Monks Orchard Estate on the Beckenham border and was opened on its new site by H.M. Queen Mary.

Beckenham has had three almshouses since 1694 when Anthony Rawlins left a bequest of £50 so that these might be built. They are still in use at the side of the parish church.

47. The Anthony Rawlins almshouses before they were modernised in the 1880s.

The presence of the Crystal Palace, a major electrical factory (Muirheads), and a large wealthy population resulted in Beckenham Council adopting a very forward thinking attitude to the production and use of electricity in the parish. The local board first applied for an Electric Lighting Order for the parish in 1882 but this was only to thwart an application by a private company and was not pursued. The board did nothing until 10 years later, when the Crystal Palace and District Electric Lighting Supply Company, based just outside the parish in Sydenham, obtained an order which included the Lawrie Park part of Beckenham. It must be remembered that at this time even gas lighting was a luxury which only the well-off could afford. Beckenham got its own order in 1893 and the generating station, situated at the depot in Churchfields Road, opened on 22 November 1900, consuming the town's refuse as part of its fuel, one of the first examples of practical re-cycling.

48. This electricity power station, situated off Arthur Road, was opened by the council in 1900. It used water from the nearby stream for cooling and domestic rubbish as part of its fuel.

An electricity showroom was opened in 1910 on the corner of Manor Road, where it remained until moving into magnificent purpose-built premises, an integral part of the new Town Hall in 1932. Beckenham lost control of the undertaking on nationalisation in 1948, although long before this supplies had been taken from the national grid and local generation had been abandoned. The showroom was closed soon after the London Electricity Board was privatised and in 1992 it was demolished to make way for a Marks & Spencer food store.

The first large-scale practical use of electricity was for communication. The electric telegraph came to Beckenham with the railways, but passed into the control of the post office in 1869 when it was gradually made available at all major post offices. The telephone appeared surprisingly early. Beckenham was initially served from the National Telephone Company's exchange in Bromley which opened sometime before 1890 and was renamed Ravensbourne in 1924 to avoid confusion with Croydon when automatic dialling was introduced. Beckenham got its own exchange, which is still in use, in July 1928.

Whilst Beckenham was a tiny village the churchyard at the parish church had been adequate, but as the population increased it became obvious that further ground would be needed. The extension of the churchyard in 1868 only helped for a very short time, and in 1876 the Elmers End cemetery opened. Beckenham churchyard was closed for burials in 1890, except for families with existing rights some of which are still valid, e.g. Rob Copeland, at the present day.

The Crystal Palace and District Cemetery Co. Ltd., now called Birkbeck Securities Ltd., traces its origins back to the London and Suburban Land and Building Society set up in 1852 as one of the associations whose aims were to acquire land and thus obtain a vote under the 1832 Reform Act. It became a limited company in 1863 and five years later purchased 41 acres at

CRYSTAL PALACE DISTRICT CEMETERY CO;

(LIMITED)

ELMER'S END ROAD, BECKENHAM, S.E.

Between Anerley and Elmers End Railway Stations.

ELIGIBLE
FRONTAGE
SITES
FOR THE
DISPLAY OF
MONUMENTS
AND
INSCRIPTIONS
MAY BE SECURED
AT
MODERATE CHARGES.

ORDINARY
INTERMENTS
FROM
$150

PRIVATE GRAVES
FROM
$330
UPWARDS.

ADJACENT TO PENGE, SYDENHAM, FOREST HILL,
THORNTON HEATH, BROMLEY, GIPSY HILL, TULSE HILL, CROYDON, ADDISCOMBE, NORWOOD,
and convenient to the **SOUTH OF LONDON** generally.

The Cemetery Grounds are open to the Public on Week Days from 9.30 till Sunset, and on Sundays from 2 to 5 p.m.
All Particulars relating to Interment Fees, &c., can be obtained of the SECRETARY, at the

OFFICE—CEMETERY, ELMERS END ROAD, S.E.

49. Elmers End cemetery poster can still be seen in the cemetery office, and clearly depicts the rural nature of the area.

Elmers End from William Cator for £12,000. In 1870 it was decided that use of the site for a cemetery would be a good investment and outline approval from the Secretary of State was obtained. In order to develop the site and meet the governmental and religious requirements, a new company was formed in 1873. It is believed that this is the oldest commercial cemetery company in the country. The last war brought to an end nearly seventy years of increasing trade and prosperity, so in the 1950s the company diversified into cremations. One of the original chapels was converted into a crematorium in 1956 and its capacity doubled in 1960. Ten years later the company name was changed to Beckenham Crematorium Ltd., and in 1979 to its present title. The cemetery services a wide area, not only Beckenham. It contains the graves of a number of distinguished people including Thomas Crapper the famous Victorian plumber, W. G. Grace, the cricketer, and Wolseley, the car manufacturer.

Both the London and Provincial and the London and Counties Banks opened branches in Beckenham in 1874, the former in a chemist's shop run by the local postmaster. Within ten years the two rivals had moved into purpose-built premises, the former now part of Barclays, on the corner of Rectory Road where it operated for 108 years, and the latter, now part of National Westminster, on the corner of Bromley Road where it remains to the present day. In 1898 the Midland Bank opened on the corner of Mackenzie Road where it stayed until 1962, when it moved to Penge. It was 1925 before the Midland was represented in central Beckenham followed three years later by Lloyds.

50. The London & Provincial Bank on the corner of Rectory Road, *c.*1910. This bank, now part of Barclays, opened in Beckenham in 1874 and operated from this site, formerly part of the rectory garden, for 108 years.

51. Roger's grocers shop and post office in the High Street, 1869. At the introduction of uniform penny postage in 1840, Beckenham's only post office was here. Letters arrived and departed by mailcart to and from London four times a day.

52. Beckenham's main post office in 1897 was decorated for the Queen's golden jubilee just before it moved to the new building further up Albemarle Road.

   The development of the postal service is yet another indication of the quickening pulse of activity in an area. Beckenham's first pillar box was in Park Road but cannot be the present one which is of 1887-1904 vintage. By 1866, the postmaster was listed as Richard East, Beckenham village. Three years later Thomas Sweeting Day, the chemist near Beckenham Junction had become the postmaster. Beckenham was now a post town addressed as Beckenham, Kent and not Beckenham S.E. as previously. By the late 1870s the post office had moved around the corner to Mrs. Peverill's stationery shop. In later years this became a crown post office. In 1897 a purpose-built office was opened in Albemarle Road on the site now occupied by St George's parish church hall. It remained there until 1939 when the present main post office took over. Beckenham by then had five sub-offices and nine pillar boxes. The sub-offices are listed as High Street, Bromley Road, Avenue Road Birkbeck, Kent House, and Elmers End.

   In the *Beckenham Journal*, Jubilee Edition of 1936, a Mrs. Town, then 89 years of age, relates a story concerning the mail cart at a time when, according to her, there was no post office in the place, the mail being left at the police station. According to Pigot there was a post office in 1835 and the police station did not appear until 1839, so this cannot be strictly true. The story was that the driver had frozen to death in his cart and the horse pulled up outside and waited until the police came out to investigate. A Mr. Glover, who was then 84, states that in his youth there were he, fancies, only about three postmen (and about three policemen which we know to be wrong); the mail was sent to and from Bromley by road. The driver of the mail cart announced his arrival at the post office by sounding his horn. He pins down the approximate date by describing the station as a terminus with a turntable.

53. The new post office and sorting office in 1897. The purpose-built office is seen here with its builders. When the post office closed in 1939 the building was used for a succession of other businesses.

Chapter IV

Transport

Rail, Public and Private Road Transport and Associated Trades

Improvements in transport have had more influence on the development of Beckenham than any other factor. The town's initial combination of nearness to London and remoteness from a main road encouraged larger estates which changed once the village had its own direct rail service.

Beckenham's first public transport was a twice-weekly coach service to London, started in 1715 when the roads resembled what we today would regard as cart tracks, dusty in summer, rutted and almost impassable in bad weather. They were the responsibility of the local vestry, apart from the route from Lewisham to Croydon, which in 1765 was under the care of the New Cross Turnpike Trust. By 1839, a coach named *The Accommodation* was running every morning to London and returning the same day. Later, when Sydenham station on the London to Croydon Railway opened, William Legg who lived at Elm Cottage, on the corner of what is now Village Way, started an omnibus service to meet the trains; this was later taken over by William Ovenden, the licensee of *The Three Tuns*. By 1855, just before the village got its own station, an omnibus was running four times daily, starting from *The White Hart* in Bromley.

The London to Croydon Railway replaced the canal of the same name which had opened in 1809 and closed in 1836. Both the canal and the railway passed through the north-west corner of Beckenham parish affording a modest revenue to the vestry which assessed the latter at £9 in 1839. In 1854 a branch line was built, passing through the parish, to serve the newly opened Crystal Palace. By this time work by the West London & Crystal Palace Railway to construct a branch from London Bridge to Beckenham via New Cross and Catford was well under way. Beckenham station opened in January 1857, making it older than most of the present London termini. Within a year a single line extension had been built to Shortlands to serve Bromley, and an alternative route constructed to London via Crystal Palace. Beckenham station was renamed Beckenham Junction and its turntable removed.

In 1863, what had become the London, Chatham & Dover Railway opened a more direct line to London through a tunnel under Sydenham Hill and with a station called Penge East which, despite its name, was in Beckenham. The following year the South Eastern Railway, which had by now absorbed the Mid-Kent Company, started a line to the east side of Croydon with stations at New Beckenham and Elmers End. Thus in seven years the bulk of the complex rail system which now serves all parts of the parish had been created. The only later additions were the Hayes branch, opened in 1882, and the Shortlands to Nunhead railway 10 years later. Rapid development in the north of the parish resulted in the subsequent opening of three more stations. Kent House station in 1884, Clock House station in 1890, and finally Birkbeck which did not open until March 1930. Many of the early stations were built in what was then open country in anticipation of rapid building development in the vicinity, but this did not always take place. The first New Beckenham station closed after two years when it was found that there

54. Beckenham station. Michael Moore, Beckenham's first stationmaster, poses in 1864 when the station was completely roofed over. The woodwork was painted white and the ironwork red with the bolts picked out in blue. Its gardens were tended by Cator estate employees.

55. New Beckenham station in 1993. A level crossing, which was situated where the pedestrian underpass is now, was closed in 1900 when Bridge Road was opened and the station itself rebuilt in stages finishing in 1904.

56. Shortlands' station forecourt, *c*.1914. A stationmaster's house at this time occupied the present car park site.

was insufficient traffic to justify separate services to Addiscombe and Beckenham. This division is the reason for the wide spacing of the platforms. Originally there was a third track to enable engines to link up when the Beckenham and Addiscombe portions were separated. Lower Sydenham station on the same line was once outside the parish and moved to its present position in 1906. The lines all crossed the Cator's Beckenham estate and were constructed with the active involvement of the Cators and other big landowners who provided land and access on very favourable terms. The owners were concerned that such provision did not reduce the value and amenity of their estates and placed restrictions on the operating companies, particularly that trains should not stop at stations on the estate during divine service on Sundays.

At first the railways prospered, as they provided the best means of travel for the rapidly growing population of businessmen who needed to reach their offices in the city each day. Beckenham trains, it was said, were famous for having passengers standing in the first class whilst the second- and third-class compartments were nearly empty! Nevertheless the subjects of the many letters of complaint which filled the newspapers of the day seem very similar to the ones we read today. The trains did improve when the system was electrified in 1925, soon after the formation of the Southern Railway.

The first threat to the trains came from the electric trams which very nearly reached Beckenham. In 1902 an attempt to get a bill through Parliament authorising a line from Penge to Thornton's Corner, straightening up the High Street in the process, met violent opposition from the residents who felt it would lower the tone of the place. In 1905 the council, taking the view that trams were inevitable, succeeded in getting its own tramway bill through Parliament, but the project foundered as terms could not be agreed with the contractors. So from 1906 until 1936 trams ran through Penge, powered by electricity supplied by Beckenham, but stopping at Thicket Road, near the Beckenham boundary.

57. Beckenham Junction and a steam train, c.1912. A typical scene in the days of steam. Milk churns from the local farms can be seen awaiting despatch.

58. Despite its name Penge East station is in Beckenham but ironically Beckenham Hill is in Lewisham. The date of the picture is c.1905.

HOME AGAIN.

59. These commuters stroll up Barnmead Road from Kent House station in the evening although in the morning they had run to catch their trains.

60. Even today Ravensbourne station, seen here *c.*1900, is approached from an unmade section of a Cator estate road and still has a very rural look about it.

61. 'The Beckenham Horse Bus' early this century. The driver collected the fares through a hole in the roof and also controlled access by using his foot to operate the catch on the door.

From about 1895 until January 1914 the route which the trams would have taken was served by Tilling's Shortlands to Penge horse bus, popularly known as 'Noah's Ark'. Thomas Tilling, who had started his business in 1847 with one horse, dominated the South London transport scene at this time. His company had two depots in Beckenham, one at the side of the *Oakhill Tavern* and another beside the *Railway Hotel* in the High Street.

In Victorian times people of consequence in Beckenham would own horses and in most cases employed a coachman as well. So numerous were these employees in the town that they could raise a cricket team to play the gardeners. At this time people thought nothing of walking several miles and with no less than 12 railway stations within the parish the lack of a good public bus system was not the disadvantage it would be today.

In 1896 it became legal for the first time to drive a vehicle weighing less than three tons on the public highway without the need for someone to walk in front to warn other road users of its approach. The obligation of this person to carry a red flag had already been removed in 1878. Tilling started to motorise his bus services in 1904 and the Shortlands to Penge route was one of the last to be converted. The last horse bus ran at 11.30 p.m. on 3 January 1914 but it was not until 1 June that the 112 motor bus service from the *White Hart*, Bromley to Thicket Road, Penge started. The following month service 113, Beckenham Junction to Park Langley, also commenced, both services using vehicles based at Catford Garage. They ceased abruptly on the outbreak of war as all the buses were requisitioned for military duties. The service was resumed as No. 109 and extended to Woolwich in the latter half of the war to provide transport for munitions workers at the Arsenal. It was suspended once the war ended and the need for munitions work ceased but, after protests, it resumed in September 1919 with a terminus at Bromley North, extended to Chislehurst six months later.

62. A service 109 bus outside the parish church in the 1920s. After the war the number and variety of bus services grew rapidly and by 1935 no less than 85 buses a day were passing through Beckenham High Street. In 1934 the newly formed London Passenger Transport Board did away with the old police numbering system and the 109 Penge to Bromley service seen here acquired its familiar 227 route number.

63. Elmers End bus garage in 1937. This garage received a direct hit by a V1 rocket during the war and many of its buses were destroyed in the ensuing fire. Eighteen people lost their lives in this incident.

There were several tollgates on the approaches to the Cator estate until the turn of the century. The one at Kent House Farm existed until 1883 and that in Lennard Road, opposite Holy Trinity church, was removed in 1894. The nearest tollgate to Beckenham is now at Dulwich near to the college, and the charge for a car has recently been increased to fifty pence.

By the 1880s bicycles were an important and fashionable means of transport. The earliest mention of a cycle dealer in Beckenham in the surviving directories is that of Walter Bourdon & Co. of Station Approach in 1890. There are almost certainly earlier traders for J. W. Tostevin of the Kelsey Cycle Works claimed 24 year's experience in 1903, though this may not all have been in Beckenham. By 1914 seven dealers are listed, three of whom also claimed to be motor engineers. Garages were initially extensions of existing businesses such as blacksmiths, coach builders or cycle dealers, and only gradually specialised in the motor trade. For example, Mr. Padbury whose forge next door to the Old Wood House in the High Street, features prominently on many postcards, was by 1914 advertising that he also repaired, painted and upholstered motors at a depot three doors from the public hall, i.e. next door to the fire station. Likewise Mr. Tostevin of the Kelsey Cycle Works not only dealt in pedal cycles and repaired perambulators, mail carts and bath chairs but also supplied motor cycles. This made sense for not only was the early motor business very much a cottage industry, but servicing horse drawn traffic remained by far the more important activity until well after the end of the First World War.

G. W. Clarke made the 'Beckenham' cycle and advertised himself as a Cycle and General Engineer and sole agent for Humber, Singer, Enfield and Triumph cycles. He also sold petrol and is presumably the same man who is listed in the 1914 directory as a motor engineer with premises at 1 Wickham Road, which in 1926 were occupied by Saunders & Abbott. His 1902 address was at the side of the Conservative Club, later occupied by John Pillin, also a motor engineer.

The Siren Motor Works is listed at 59a High Street, a former builder's yard situated between Howard's Stores and *The George*. This company developed into the Beckenham Motor Co. with extensive premises, including garaging for 50 cars, situated further down the High Street between Hitt's Stores and Burrell Row.

James T. Batten who lived in Cedars Road later ran the Beckenham Motor Co. at 181 High Street. It was here that he built so many of his 'specials', which were constructed for hill climbs and trials during the 1920s. Batten and his friend and colleague, Chalenor Barson, son of a Penge Congregational minister, were often to be seen and heard driving these strange hybrids, dressed in overalls and back to front cap and goggles. The outbreak of hostilities caused the company to be wound up in March 1940. Soon afterwards James Batten was engaged in secret development work for the army and in post-war years he worked with the Rootes Group.

The Beckenham Motor Works closed sometime after the end of the last war but a firm that is still with us is Saunders and Abbott. Like many early motor businesses, Ambrose James Saunders started as a cycle dealer. We first read of him in Station Approach in 1917, and by 1919 he had teamed up with Mr. Abbott and was occupying both Tilling's old depot at the side of the *Station Hotel* and a shed adjoining the fire station in Bromley Road. (It may be due to this close proximity that the fire brigade acquired a motor cycle fire engine.) About 1926 the firm moved from the fire station to the old established garage in Wickham Road now called 'Autobahn'. Originally Price's Bedding Factory, this garage was founded by George Clarke, another cycle dealer turned motor engineer, who had been succeeded about 1912 by R. & H. Kilner. Saunders collapsed and died outside the *William IV* public house in Elmers End during the war and his surviving partner sold the Wickham Road site to a Mr. Harry Epps in 1956.

64. Three production Batten Specials, *c*.1937. The one on the left of the picture being the last of these cars, a coupé specially built for Lord Plunket.

65. Beckenham war memorial, *c*.1925. When it was erected in 1921 the town's war memorial stood in splendid isolation in the middle of the road and traffic passed on either side.

66. Beckenham's first roundabout, seen here in the early '30s. The roundabout at the war memorial was constructed in 1930 and the 'Keep Left One Way Only' sign was temporarily fixed to the lamp post.

67. The Chinese Garage and forecourt soon after opening, *c*.1920. The filling station was run to an unusually high standard with attendants dressed in plum-coloured chauffeur's outfits. When the service bay was added, a taxi service was started to take customers to the station whilst their cars were being attended to.

68. John Pillin's garage. The door of the vehicle outside the garage has 'By Appointment' on it so it is possible that it belonged to Haggers the butchers.

Private cars were soon a common sight in the village and reports of motor accidents and speeding became commonplace. In its annual report for 1912, the Cottage Hospital commented on the dramatic rise in the number of casualties treated, 1,026 compared with 285 the previous year, due to the increase in motor traffic. The High Street was surfaced for the first time in 1905 and between the wars virtually the whole of the lower section from Thornton's Corner to the war memorial was widened and partly straightened. The 1896 Act laid down a general speed limit of 14 m.p.h. which was increased to 20 m.p.h. in 1903. The present 30 m.p.h. limit in built-up areas dates from the Hore-Belisha Act of 1934 which also authorised the well-known pedestrian crossings.

In 1930 the Ministry of Transport proposed that what was termed a 'merry go round' one-way system be introduced where the Croydon Road joined Beckenham Road, and the council suggested that the war memorial be re-sited in a more tranquil position either at Thornton's Corner or in Croydon Road Recreation Ground. The Thornton's Corner site, which had been acquired by the council from the post office when they erected the telephone exchange, was already earmarked for a public lavatory but, more importantly, popular opinion was very much against moving the memorial so in the end it was decided to allow it to remain whilst enlarging and landscaping the new traffic island to provide a more suitable setting. Two other roundabouts in the town, one by the Chinese Garage on the Wickham Road and the other at Elmers End Green, were constructed about the same time. Automatic traffic lights were first installed at each end of Manor Road in the mid 1930s.

Between the wars and before the High Street reached its present congested state there were at least three other places along its length where one could stop and purchase petrol. John Pillin had a garage by the side of the Constitutional Club, Christ Church had leased its newly acquired site in the centre of the High Street to a Mr. H. N. Thomson on condition he did not trade on Sundays, and a Mr. Dineen sold motor cycles and petrol from a shop still called Deen's Garage just round the corner in Croydon Road.

69. This shop in Croydon Road was owned by a Mr. Dineen who ran a motor car hire service for many years. The petrol pump on the pavement outside did not disappear until long after the last war.

Chapter V

Education

Primary, Secondary and Private

Education was closely tied to the church in early times and we read in the *Life of the learned Dr. Assheton, Rector of Beckenham 1677-1711*, that the Doctor, 'began to raise a Charity School'. Records do not show where the school was nor how long it continued, but it was probably abandoned at the death of the Rector, or shortly afterwards, as not long after that date we read of children being sent to the master of the village workhouse to receive elementary education.

In 1717 Captain Leonard Bowyer bequeathed £100 to the parish, the interest of which was to be used for teaching four boys belonging to the parish to read and write. For many years, the master of the workhouse received the income of this fund and taught children sent to him by the churchwardens. This was still being done in 1819.

Mary Watson, who died in 1795, left most of her personal estate to the church, on which went the interest to pay for the teaching to read and write of so many poor people of Beckenham as were not maintained or supported by the parish.

The Church of England 'National Society for Educating the Poor' and the British and Foreign School Society were both founded at the beginning of the 19th century. Under these two societies, a number of so-called 'National' and 'British' schools were gradually established in England. The school in Bromley Road, originally known as the National School, was built on a field by St George's church, given by John B. Cator, the Lord of the Manor. In addition to the gift of the site, he also provided materials for building a garden around the school, and out of work parishioners were employed in levelling the ground and laying out this garden. The work was commenced in April 1818, and the school, a small two-roomed building, opened six months later with 36 boys and 36 girls, most of whom were the children of workers on the local estates. There was a resident schoolmaster and schoolmistress to teach them.

At a meeting of the school board in 1876 it was proposed that additional school accommodation was needed for children in the Alexandra District. There was already a national school in this area but it was exceedingly unpopular and it was said that many parents were sending their children to private schools or to St John's school in Penge, rather than to the existing one which was in such a deplorable state. Mr. Albemarle Cator had originally given the land on which the school was built and later he also passed over the buildings to the school board.

The national system of education dates from Gladstone's Education Act of 1870, which established school boards all over the country to provide primary education for children between the ages of five and 12 years. This made it possible for the first time to use public funds to provide elementary education. Beckenham became a school district in 1875, and the Beckenham School Board was formed. Although the act required children to start school at the age of five, a compulsory leaving age had not been established. Directly pupils had learned something of the three R's their parents wanted them to leave school and get a job, although they might only be 11 years old.

70. St James's School next to the church, c.1890. The surroundings were idyllic, with a little stream running through the grounds, large trees which gave shade for outdoor summer lessons, and the lowing cattle could be heard on the adjacent farm.

The little St James's School at Elmers End was opened in 1880 behind the new church. There are still several people living in the district who attended this school before it closed in May 1930 and all have very happy memories of their time spent there. Miss Hayes, who started teaching there in 1911 is still alive in 1993 at 102 years of age and still maintains a keen interest in the area and especially in Marian Vian School which superceded the little church school in 1930.

In 1889 the Trustees of the Churchfields Charity in 1889 sold part of Bellrope Field to the Beckenham School Board and a school known as Arthur Road School was opened a year later. The name of the road and the school was changed to Churchfields, after the charity from which the ground had been purchased. The school had four buildings—infants, juniors, seniors and a special department. The senior boys later went to Alexandra School and the senior girls stayed until the secondary schools re-organisation in 1946, when the pupils were transferred to Marian Vian or Melvin Road in Penge. The special department closed and the building was used as an adult art centre.

71. Churchfields Road School, c.1910. Note the tiered rows towards the back of the classroom.

72. The Technical Institute, c.1914. The catchment area before 1914 was very wide. In 1905, 42 per cent of the boys came from outside the bounds of Beckenham. They came from Penge, of course, but also from Sydenham and in the Bromley direction, as far afield as Downe. The Bromley County Secondary School did not open until 1911.

In 1989, just before its centenary, the school was transferred to a new building on the allotments behind the refuse tip in Churchfields Road, which caused many heated protests at the time from parents and local residents. The old site was redeveloped for housing.

Although Gladstone's Act of 1870 had provided education for children up to the age of 12 years, the Beckenham School Board had no power to spend public money on secondary schooling. It is an unfortunate fact that, throughout the 19th century, Britain, although at that time by far the richest nation in the world, was content to leave the initiative for providing secondary education almost entirely to private enterprise. However, under The Technical Instruction Act of 1889 it became possible to use public funds for secondary education, and it was decided to build the Beckenham Technical Institute in Beckenham Road. The site, a gift from Albemarle Cator, occupied the exact site of the old Clock House, which had been demolished only a few years previously. The foundation stone was laid in July 1899 and the building was formally opened on 4 June 1901. The Institute consisted of the School of Art, the Boys' Day School and the Evening Classes.

The population of Beckenham was only about 20,000 when the school was built and the districts of Eden Park and Elmers End were still open fields or private park land. The shops on Clock House Parade near the station had not been built and the Chaffinch brook flowed through a wooded dell where the boys often played. Clock House Road only ran for a very short distance and then ended in fields through which a footpath ran to Elmers End station. The main road from Beckenham to Penge, onto which the school faced, was, even in those days, busy with traffic. There were closed horse buses which followed the route of the present-day No.227. The traffic in Beckenham Road was disrupted twice a day by cows being driven from Ousley's Dairy in Sidney Road to and from the grazing fields at the end of Clock House Road.

The Beckenham Baths were opened in 1901 and, shortly afterwards, owing largely to the efforts of Dr. Randell, a member of the council, swimming was made a compulsory subject in the elementary schools of Beckenham—the first area in the country where this requirement was made. Beckenham had had another first when in 1896 the school board attracted considerable attention throughout England, having decided that the Union Jack should be hoisted on all the elementary schools on special occasions.

Balfour's Education Act of 1902 changed the status of the school because it placed full responsibility for providing secondary education on the county councils. Beckenham, by establishing the Day School, had in a sense anticipated the act. The Beckenham Technical Day School became the Beckenham County Secondary School, the first of its kind in the county of Kent, and possibly in the country.

Fees were charged, and to begin with they were £1 15s. per term for sons of Beckenham ratepayers and £2 2s. for others. From the start there had been 16 scholarship places awarded by the Local Authority, but from 1907 it became obligatory to provide 25 per cent free places in all maintained county secondary schools. These were competed for in an annual scholarship examination and fee-payers also had to pass an entrance examination. This remained the system of entry until 1944.

Baden Powell founded the Boy Scout movement in 1907 and, shortly after this, the technical school formed a troop under the leadership of Mr. R. W. Clark. It was the 1st Beckenham Troop and grew to a membership of about fifty. However, as other troops connected with the churches began to appear, the numbers in the school troop started to decline and it was disbanded.

Once the war was over, the local authorities began to look for a site to build a larger school. The St Arvan's site in Penge was acquired in 1925 and building commenced in 1929. The school remained at Penge until January 1968, when it was transferred to the new larger buildings at Eden Park and was renamed Langley Park School for Boys.

73. The County School for Boys, Beckenham and Penge, c.1935. The new school, a few yards across the Beckenham border, was ready for occupation at the beginning of 1931. Mr. Sidney Gammon, a graduate in history from New College, Oxford, became headmaster in the autumn term that year and remained until he was killed along with his wife and son in a bombing raid on 23 October 1940.

74. Miss Fox and the prefects in 1924. Pupils had to wear black stockings both summer and winter, and the square-necked blouses ensured that necks were washed daily! Gym slips had to be a regulation four inches above the knees.

75. Lennard Road staff in 1946. The staff in Miss Fox's day were expected to wear dresses or blouses with high necks and long sleeves. Dress became less formal after the war.

After 1931, when the school moved to Penge, the building in Beckenham Road was used as a technical school until this moved to new buildings in Bromley in 1955. It was then taken over by the Alexandra Secondary School for Boys until they in turn moved to their new building near Kelsey Park in 1968, when it became an Adult Evening Centre.

It had soon become obvious that more secondary schools were required, and it was decided to build two more. Lennard Road was to become the Beckenham County School for Girls, whilst the Balgowan Road School became a combined Boys' and Girls' Central School, the first co-ed school in Kent. The First World War had started before either of the new schools were opened and the buildings were requisitioned as Red Cross Military Hospitals. They were returned to the education committee in 1919 and opened for their original purpose in September of that year.

Miss Fox was headmistress at Lennard Road for the first 24 years. Her pupils were known as 'Miss Fox's young ladies'. She was an extremely strict disciplinarian both with the staff as well as with the children. Miss Fox retired just before the end of the Second World War and the atmosphere became considerably more relaxed. No longer were the staff expected to wear long skirts, long sleeves, and high necks. The pupils wore beige lisle stockings instead of the original black ones and the younger girls were allowed ankle socks—a great concession while clothes rationing was still in operation.

One of the really significant changes in council-provided education concerned the development of secondary schools. Under Fisher's Education Act of 1918 a duty was imposed on local authorities to provide secondary schools in which at least 20 per cent of the places were to be free. This was not intended to mean secondary education for everyone, but rather for those who, regardless of financial circumstances, showed they could benefit from it. Right up to 1945 the majority of children still attended full-time schooling at elementary schools to the age of 14—raised from 13 under Fisher's Act.

At the beginning of the century most boys' scholastic ambition was London Matriculation at the age of 16, and very few stayed on at school after this. There has been a vast expansion in the sixth form since those days. Many were going on to university but, until the introduction of state grants for students, it had not been easy for average County School children to go to university unless they could win a major scholarship. Another important development in education came about as a result of a need to provide less academic children with a more 'practical' kind of secondary school. This was called the Central School, which laid emphasis on commercial training, technical training, music and art. The name disappeared after the Second World War but the concept lived on under the guise of the Secondary Technical School.

The boys' school at Kent House Road became Kent Wood Secondary Modern School for Boys, then Royston Primary School and is now partly used as an adult education centre. The Lennard Road site became Cator Park Secondary Modern School for Girls. Balgowan Central had its boys' section closed after the re-organisation of schools within the borough in 1946. The girls' section was extended to take girls from Bromley Road and other schools and continued there as a Secondary Modern School until it moved to the empty Lennard Road building in 1959.

The girls' secondary school at Marian Vian became a mixed school known as Spring Park Lower until it finally closed in July 1979. That building is now an adult education centre. The junior mixed and infant departments of Marian Vian became a joint primary school in 1982 and in 1992 celebrated its Diamond Jubilee.

Stewart Fleming Primary School opened in September 1939 to take the children living near Birkbeck station; it was named after the Rev. Stewart Fleming who, whilst minister at Elm Road Baptist Church, was for many years chairman of the Beckenham School Board.

76. The Hall in Bromley Road was probably built by the Cator family in the 18th century, but very little is known of its early history. Peter Cator, who played a prominent part in the development of the Cator Estate, lived there until his death in 1873. In 1878 Charles Cator was in residence. A school was started there in 1893 and St Christopher's took over in 1926 and celebrated its centenary in 1993.

77. The dormitory at Raymont School, Shortlands, *c*.1910. Raymont school off Bromley Road was a small boarding school for girls.

78. Minshull House, in Park Road, *c*.1910. One of the oldest private schools in the area, it was established well before the turn of the century. The school was evacuated to Woolacombe in Devon during the Second World War and there were specially reduced war-time fees. In 1965 it was pulled down and redeveloped for residential purposes.

79. Kepplestone School, c.1908. The rear view of the school in Overbury Avenue just before the First World War.

80. An advert for a bazaar at Kepplestone, in 1905 (on the right). The bazaar was held while the school was still at Kelsey Manor. The exorbitant entrance fee of 1s. would have kept many of Beckenham's population away, for the majority of working-class men's wages were less than £2 per week in those days.

In the late Victorian and Edwardian times private schools of all shapes and sizes were so numerous in Beckenham that it would not be out of place to describe education as a most important commercial undertaking. It was an occupation which appeared very early in the development of the town. Many were too small to survive. At one time there were eight in Mackenzie Road alone. However, of the larger ones, some of which were also boarding schools, several have survived and are still thriving today.

The well-known girls' school, St Christopher's, opened in Perth Road in 1893, then, after two changes of address, merged in 1926 with another school at The Hall, Bromley Road. Enid Blyton was perhaps St Christopher's most famous pupil. She attended between 1907 and 1917 and was a prize winner in 1915.

Other girls' schools were Raymont in Shortlands Grove, run by the Kendall sisters, Minshull House at 3 Park Road, Beckenham, and Kepplestone School.

Kepplestone School for the Daughters of Gentlemen was at Kelsey Manor until that building became too delapidated in 1908 when the school moved to Overbury Avenue.

Most private schools were in large houses adapted for the purpose, but the Abbey School, founded in 1866 by one of the curates at the parish church, was quite exceptional. Starting over Leven's the baker's shop in the High Street, it soon moved to a gravel pit on 16 acres of the old Copers Cope Farm, and until its closure enjoyed a notable reputation for getting its boys into public schools and the Royal Navy. It could claim at least one holder of the Victoria Cross among its former pupils. This was Lt. John Norwood, born at Pembury Lodge, Beckenham in 1876, who won the V.C. at Ladysmith, but was killed in action in France in the First World War.

81. The Abbey School, in Southend Road, *c*.1910. The buildings were purpose-built and in the dormitories each boy had a separate cubicle. By the 1930s central heating and electric light were installed throughout. The grounds provided ample playing fields and there was a riding school attached.

82. One of the football pitches at the Abbey School, *c*.1910. The extensive grounds enabled the school to have more than one pitch for their soccer matches.

83. Clare House School in Oakwood Avenue. The message on the reverse of this card, posted in 1906, reads 'Hope you all got back safely from the station without meeting the ticket collector. Love from Dad.' Presumably the writer could afford to send his sons to a private school but not to pay their dues to the railway company!

84. Craven College in Dunbar Avenue just before the First World War. There was a fine polo ground at the rear which was said to be one of the finest in the country.

Some schools simply closed down during the war years, Clare House at 22 Oakwood Avenue, Beckenham being a case in point. This school, which was founded in 1896, took boys as day or boarding pupils, and prepared them to enter a public school or the Royal Navy. It finally failed in 1970 owing to financial difficulties, but the name is carried on by a school in the state sector which opened on the same site.

Bishop Challoner is an independent Catholic day school in Bromley Road, Shortlands and caters for children from two years to 18 years. It uses the old Shortlands House and was opened in 1950.

Elmer Lodge near the junction of Dunbar Avenue and Eden Park Avenue, where the magistrate Edward Adams once lived, was at one time Craven College Boys' School.

Albemarle College, founded in 1879 at 10 Beckenham Road as a girls' school, was reorganised in 1930 as a modern secretarial and tutorial college. Courses of secretarial and commercial training were provided for students of both sexes with previous high school or public school education. Coaching was given for Professional and Civil Service Examinations.

The Grange Preparatory School for Boys, 25 Wickham Road, founded in 1926, prepared boys from the ages of seven to 14 for all public schools. There was a separate junior department for boys of five to seven years. The classrooms were lofty and well-ventilated, and they had a large sports ground, near Park Langley. In 1930 the school prospectus advertised 'large sports ground in Open Country'.

Irene ↓   *Muriel* ↓

ST OLAFS SCHOOL   BECKENHAM

↑ *Molly*   ↑ *Thelma*

85. St Olaf's school at 2 Cedars Road around 1910. This small mixed school obviously catered for all ages and whole families were sent there, as can be seen by the four sisters indicated by arrows.

Woodbrook, in Hayne Road, was a school run on the most up-to-date lines, providing for the education of children from nursery to college. The rooms were large and airy; there was a large garden for work and games, and a sandpit for the little ones. There was a nursery department which provided educational occupations for children under five, and the work from kindergarten up was carefully graded. Individual attention was given to each child and, to ensure this, the classes were kept small. The principals were especially interested in the 'backward' child. Very successful work was done in preparing pupils for advanced examinations. Senior girls were prepared for the Oxford school certificate and London Matriculation, and boys for entrance to public and preparatory schools. The most modern methods were adopted throughout the school. There was a laboratory, gymnasium, and garden. Hockey, netball, tennis and swimming were taught.

St Olaf's school was on the corner of Cedars Road and Croydon Road. It opened at the beginning of the century but did not survive when the First World War began.

Besides these there were numerous dancing schools, secretarial and business training schools. A very successful school of art was started in 1901 at the technical institute and later was moved further along Beckenham Road opposite Elm Road. It was sadly burnt down in the early 1980s and not rebuilt. There was a branch of this school for many years at 80 Croydon Road. The school gained great prominence in examinations in art by the success of its pupils, who took some of the chief awards. There were two sections, senior and junior, and all branches of art were taught.

There was a music college in The Parade facing Beckenham Junction with an impressive list of professors. The Royal Academy of Dancing & Music was at The Studio in the High Street, Doris Nichols taught ballroom dancing at The Assembly Rooms, whilst Joan Baron held her classes at the *Eden Park Hotel*.

Adult evening classes were held at various schools in the borough and in particular at the Evening Education Centre in Beckenham Road at the old technical institute building. Many of the classes now could almost be listed under leisure rather than education for they cover such a wide selection of subjects from purely educational, the whole range of art and handicrafts, family and local history, to keeping fit and dancing.

Balfour's Act of 1901 started in this country the system of publicly maintained secondary schools, but the second great milestone in its history was R. A. Butler's Act of 1944. It made secondary education for all to the age of 15 compulsory and free and, although there was nothing in the Act to prevent county authorities from setting up comprehensive secondary schools, the general pattern was that of selection at the age of eleven-plus for either grammar, technical or modern schools. Later the eleven-plus examination was abolished and selective schools ceased to be.

In the thirties there were gradual improvements in the school health and welfare services. It was a requirement that children be medically examined three times during their school life, and, though the medicals were perfunctory affairs lasting only a few minutes and were too infrequent to spot unhealthy conditions at an early stage, they could result in treatment, however belated, that might otherwise never be given. The clinic block at the new town hall was unusual and forward looking. It was a complete child welfare and health centre and covered all ages from ante-natal care to senior school children. In 1933 about one-third of children at council schools attended school clinics. Nearly half of these were at the dental clinic. Under a newly introduced scheme children could receive daily at school one-third of a pint of fresh milk for a charge of one halfpenny (old money).

Dr. T. Phillips Cole, M.o.H. for Beckenham, reported in 1933 that too many children were underweight, 'a serious problem if it is not put right', but unemployment among parents was not seen as a significant factor in this. By 1936 the immunisation programme had reduced diphtheria cases in Beckenham to only five, against 122 for scarlet fever. By then over half of the children in local schools were taking daily milk.

What is perhaps remembered most clearly about school medical matters from those days is the regular appearances of a nurse who went through every child's head in search of lice. She was affectionately called 'Nitty Norah'.

Chapter VI

Industry and Commerce

Shops, Factories and Tradesmen

The clearest early glimpse we can get of the commercial life of Beckenham is provided by Pigot's 1839 *Kent Directory* in which 33 tradesmen are listed. Thirteen years later, when work had started on building the Crystal Palace in the parish, the population had increased by over a quarter, and about half of the original tradesmen are still in business. Notable newcomers are a surgeon, a chemist and no less than four beer retailers.

There was the West Kent brewery which opened up in Upper Elmers End Road in the mid-19th century. The going rate then for beer was, India pale ale at 1s. 6d. a gallon, stout at 1s. 4d. a gallon and 'porter' ale, just a shilling. The brewery was run by Pontiflex and Hall for 30 years and they mixed their hops in Elmers End, and were very proud of their product. Soon after their opening, they announced that they had 'sunk a deep artesian well and have much pleasure in stating that the water obtained from there is pronounced by an eminent doctor to be of the purest quality. From this water all our beers are produced'. And of the building itself they said, 'It is constructed on the most proven modern principles and is particularly adapted for the production of high-class family ales'. The brewery closed early this century and the building was taken over by Kempton's Pies. The old building was demolished in the 1960s and the site is now a block of council flats.

86. Upper Elmers End Road showing *The Rising Sun* and the brewery with its tall chimney, a little further down the road.

87. A forge in Burnhill Road, *c*.1900. The blacksmith would also sometimes make large steel hoops with which the children could play in the uncongested streets of bygone days.

Beckenham village industries were the smithies, millers, carpenters and masons. The blacksmiths, beside shoeing the horses, would repair the farm tools and machinery, and assist the local wheelwright. Farming remained an important occupation until the housing developments of the 1920s swallowed up the last remnants of open country. Until this time there were fields in the centre of Beckenham and along the Croydon Road, and it was nothing unusual for traffic to be disrupted as cows were driven from their grazing fields to the dairy.

Another local industry was brick making. There were several large brickfields in Beckenham and the surrounding areas. William Pitt introduced a tax on bricks in 1784 and immediately, to avoid this tax, bricks were made larger until in 1803 the tax was doubled if the brick was made bigger than 10 x 3 x 5 inches before firing. The size could be reduced by up to 10 per cent in the kiln. The tax was abolished in 1850. Several brickyards had opened to exploit the local clay and supply builders. The Mid-Kent Brickworks in Worsley Bridge Road hit the headlines in 1885 when five workers were killed in a boiler explosion.

Many of the businesses in the new town were started by people who came from other parts of the country, attracted by the opportunities arising from the growing population, and the active building programme. A particularly good example is that of Syme & Duncan Ltd., a firm of builders founded in 1870. James Syme was a Scotsman and skilled carpenter, employed in 1870 by a firm which was constructing St Mary's vicarage at Shortlands. The firm went into liquidation and James as foreman was asked if he could finish the job himself. This he did with the help of a friend, William Duncan, a fellow tradesman, also from Scotland. With this success behind them the partners went on to build a series of houses in Southend Road, Rectory Road and elsewhere, it is believed on a speculative basis. Before the houses were started it was necessary to dig a well, and the gravel excavated in doing this was used in the house construction. In 1885 the firm was able to lease its present premises in Blakeney Road. One of the largest of its early successes was the construction of the parade of shops at Clock House in 1904. Syme and Duncan Ltd. are unusual in having survived to the present day, thus making them one of the oldest businesses in Beckenham.

88. The parade of shops at Clockhouse, *c*.1914. Proximity to customers was not of prime importance when tradesmen were expected to wait upon the gentry, and poorer customers usually lived in humbler dwellings in the immediate vicinity. The parade was built in 1904.

89. Hitt's stores in the High Street, *c*.1904. Hitt's shop itself has changed beyond recognition but, as is so often the case, the upper storey has survived virtually unchanged to this day.

Henry Copeland, grandfather of the late Rob Copeland, the local historian, was yet another example. He came from Sleaford in Lincolnshire in 1862 with his brother William and obtained employment as a carpenter. By 1874 he was able to set up in business on his own as a builder and undertaker from premises in the High Street. In those days it was not unusual for a builder also to be the undertaker, since he had the wood for the coffins and his labourers could dig the graves. Rob Copeland was the third generation to run the business. He died in 1988 but the firm is still flourishing.

At the beginning of the last century Beckenham's few shops were small and run by tradesmen catering for the needs of the villagers. All this changed in the 1860s and '70s when Beckenham must have had the air of a boom town. To meet the needs of the rapidly growing population on the new estates, parades of shops were built between the church and station as well as at the lower end of Albemarle Road. Development was not confined to the town centre. Shopping parades were built on the main roads in places where there were already commercial premises such as Westgate and Beckenham Roads, or in the vicinity of a railway station as at Clock House.

The more typical Victorian business was small and family owned by people who at first lived over the 'shop' and usually lasted for only two or three generations. Hitt's, Wine and Spirit Merchants, is an example of this. William Hitt came from Somerset and started his business in 1864, though he first appears in the *Bromley Directory* for 1878. In 1915 he passed on the business to his son, Frederick, who retired and sold it about 1934.

Firms from outside the area opened branches in Beckenham and some of the earliest examples were branches of local businesses based in Bromley, such as Weeks, the ironmongers, and Howards, the grocers, who built the premises at present occupied by the Midland Bank. Aylings, the Bromley shoe shop founded in 1790, also opened two branches in Beckenham and only closed in 1992.

Sainsbury's was soon followed by the Home and Colonial whilst Howards was replaced by the International Stores. As the inter-war period wore on they were joined by Boots, Timothy Whites, MacFisheries, Woolworths, Dewhursts, and Montague Burtons. These were all situated along the High Street, having taken advantage of the demolition of the old domestic properties such as the Rectory, the Manor House and

90. Howards was unusual in being sited away from the station, but its example was to be followed by the first national multiple to appear, Sainsburys, which opened in 1915 in a purpose-built block erected on the site of Gordon House.

91. Sainsbury's in the High Street opened in 1915 and was built on the site of Gordon House which had stood next to the Old Wood House, still visible on the left of the picture.

92. A parade of shops in Croydon Road, *c.*1939. It was built between the new Bramerton and Whitmore Roads.

93. Eden Park shops, *c.*1934. A small parade of shops was built opposite Eden Park station to serve the new houses in Village Way, Upper Elmers End Road and Eden Way.

94. Adam's Drapery, *c*.1910. The drapers and milliners in the High Street stocked everything a good needlewoman might require and provided chairs for their many customers as well.

Village Place and the proximity of the large new housing estate being built by J. R. Davies on their former grounds.

Between the wars additional parades were built at Eden Park, Elmers End, Croydon Road and Langley Park to serve the new housing estates. They usually consisted of smallish shops designed to cater for customers within walking distance at a time before motor cars had become such a universal possession.

The old shops may not have had the efficiency of the modern supermarket but they had an atmosphere which lives on in the memory of older people. For example, Adams the drapers, where you had to bend your head and mind the step, and your money went whizzing across the shop to the cash desk on pulling the handle of the overhead railway.

A trade which was very prominent before the first war was nursery gardening. The spectacular bedding schemes which were a feature of the Crystal Palace grounds stimulated great rivalry amongst the owners of the numerous large gardens and there was a brisk trade supplying those who from lack of time or inclination had neglected their own production. Most have disappeared, but not Castle's nursery on Elmers End Road.

Beckenham is primarily a residential area with its not inconsiderable industry confined to the northern and western outskirts at Elmers End, Churchfields, Kent House Road and Lower Sydenham. Since the war London has become too expensive and congested compared with other parts of the country, and change of ownership or reorganisation has often resulted in a re-siting elsewhere. As a result the manufacturing of electrical equipment (Muirhead 1894; Small Electric Motors 1914), leather (Kohnstamm), adhesives, office equipment (Twinlock 1920), etc., which featured so prominently before the war have been replaced by trading and

95. Castle's Nursery opposite Elmers End cemetery in 1920. This family concern was founded by John Alfred Castle in 1906 through the generosity of his former employer who provided, and later sold him, both land and house. The only condition was no Sunday trading and this instruction can still be seen carved in stone by the side of the old house door.

96. Popham's General Stores around 1920. A general store on Church Hill. The tiling at the front of the shop can still be seen today.

administrative activities. For example, a much reduced Muirheads moved from Elmers End to Penge, Small Electric Motors from Churchfields Road to Lower Sydenham, whilst important new activities like Barclays Registrars are now based at Clock House.

Small Electric Motors started operations at Churchfields Road at the beginning of the First World War. They moved down from the city over a weekend by horse and cart. Apparently the cart wheels kept getting stuck in the tram lines down the Old Kent Road and at Lewisham. The premises they took over were originally a pin and needle factory and for years afterwards these were being swept off the floor. They now operate from Kangley Bridge Road, just inside the Beckenham boundary.

Percy Jones & Co., makers of ribbons, carbons and filing systems, started Twinlock loose-leaf ledgers in Cheapside in 1910 and moved to Elmers End in 1920, next to Muirheads. These two businesses between them employed a huge work force and it was a sad day for the district when they moved away.

The Wellcome Foundation, one of the most important drug manufacturers in the world, was founded in 1880 by two American pharmacists. The company bought Langley Court in South Eden Park Road in 1921 and opened their research laboratories on the site.

97. Aerial view of the Elmers End industrial site. Taken in the 1980s it shows the Muirhead and Twinlock factories now awaiting redevelopment. The building in the centre foreground was for many years Ackerman's bakery.

98. Thornton's Corner, *c*.1913. Their sun blinds show how diverse were the services they offered and indicate why the area is now called Thornton's Corner.

Publishing in Beckenham is synonymous with the Thornton family. Thomas W. Thornton was the owner of the stationers and booksellers business on the corner of the High Street which bears his name. He purchased the *Beckenham Journal* from its founder, William Malyon, who lived in Victor Road on the Alexandra estate. He was a director of the London printers, Malyon & Watson, who are assumed to have printed the early editions of the newspaper which first appeared in September 1876.

The *Beckenham Journal* began its life as a 24-page monthly booklet costing 1d. The increasing population, as the Cator and Shortlands estates were built, in the space of one generation turned the village into a commuter town, so that by the early 1880s *The Journal* could be issued as a weekly newspaper.

Tom Thornton, who came from Norwood, walked daily to and from the Beckenham shop. He installed a steam-driven printing press behind his stationer's shop and in 1882 started to produce the paper weekly. This was later moved to a purpose-built works behind the shops on the corner of Kelsey Park and Manor Roads, editorial work being carried out in what has been described as an attached conservatory, until in 1954 one of the corner shops was acquired for the purpose.

When he died in 1933 Tom Thornton had been confined to a wheelchair for some time. He was succeeded as editor by E. J. Dark, who retired during the war, to be replaced by Victor

Thornton, who remained in the position until his death in 1963. In 1955 control of the paper was sold to the *Kentish Times*, who have continued to keep the title alive, though the printing works was almost immediately closed and production transferred to Sidcup.

The Beckenham & Penge Advertiser, an off-shoot of the *Croydon Advertiser*, also had a weekly issue.

Thornton's brought out a *Beckenham Directory* which in 1885 sold for one shilling (five pence). Besides being printers and publishers, they were listed in 1906 as stationers, billposting and advertising agents, bookbinders, newsagent, artist's colourman, fancy warehouseman, railway and steamship ticket agent, entertainment agent etc. and coped with piano tuning and picture framing. They also ran a lending library from their shop in the High Street. Beckenham did not have its own library until 1939.

Walter Andrew Mathew died aged 92 in January 1968. From 1898-1910 when he left the district, he ran Beckenham's first garage in the High Street, near *The George*, but later moved to larger premises, also in the High Street. The first motor car related businesses to be listed in the directories appear in *Thornton's Directory* for 1902—*see* chapter IV.

Holdsworth's, the well-known lightweight cycle manufacturers, started their business between the wars in Lennard Road before moving to their factory in the old banana warehouse at Lullington Road, Penge. For many years they had a shop on the corner of Barnmead Road. A range of bicycle carriers was made exclusively for the Holdsworth Co. by Tonard Brazing Co. Ltd. which started making them in Blandford Road, Beckenham in 1960 before moving to Croydon, where they became one of the largest manufacturers of cycle carriers in the country.

Ernest Walter Payne founded his jeweller's shop in Penge in 1899 and then opened a branch in Bromley market square eleven years later. The Beckenham shop in the High Street was not opened until 1932 but after over 60 years is still a thriving concern.

The Pearce family of Elmers End for many years swept the borough's chimneys before the Clean Air Act stopped coal fires. Generations of the family have been sweeping chimneys since 1640 and must surely be one of the oldest family businesses in the country. They have been much in demand to kiss brides and New Year revellers in order to bring them good luck.

David Greig the grocer lived at The Red House in Southend Road. It was unusual to have a Sainsbury's store and a David Greig's in the same area but in Beckenham there was a David Greig shop at the bottom of Mackenzie Road before it was bombed in the 1940s.

We have mentioned local farms and the milk delivery but without a doubt the United Dairies (now known as Unigate) was the most prolific. At the start of the Second World War Beckenham still had private dairies such as Ousley's, Herbert's, Ironside's and Overton's, but the United Dairies had seven shops in the borough and their distributing depot was in the High Street where the entrance to Safeway's is now. The South Suburban Co-op and the Express Dairy both delivered in the area, but the United Dairies took most of the trade. All their premises had very distinctive tiled shop fronts. Their deliveries were made by horse and cart and the horses knew the route better than many of the milkmen. If a milkman stopped for too long to talk to a customer the horse would just plod on to the next house. Because of the horses the distributing depot needed stabling, tack rooms and harness rooms, fodder lofts and a resident stable man. The vet made a weekly visit to see that all the Welsh cobs were in good condition. These horses took part in the annual Commercial Horse Parade held in Regents Park and rarely returned without several awards. The electric milk floats which we know today were introduced soon after the war ended. Fortunately Beckenham is not too hilly, because these new floats with the heavy batteries had problems when they went up hill and replacement batteries were frequently needed for them to complete the round.

99. William Leslie Simons delivering milk from the Russell Farm dairy in 1908.

100. Holdstock's the confectioner and tobacconist was at 146 Croydon Road, Beckenham and this picture was taken just before the First World War.

It is impossible to give details of the numerous businesses which have been carried on in Beckenham over the past one hundred and fifty odd years. Many were very small affairs, trading from the front room of a house, such as sweet shops and grocers in the side streets. Many women in the poorer part of the village would start up their own laundry and take in washing from the large houses at the other end of Beckenham.

Some of the larger industries are listed below although there is not room to say much about them. Stanmar Products Ltd. in Beckenham Road were dancing shoe manufacturers. J. Gardner & Co. Ltd., sheet metal & steel constructors, have now progressed to being thermal engineers and still trade from the Kent House Lane industrial site. De Vere Ltd., industrial photographic apparatus manufacturers, were at Thayers Farm Road for many years before moving out to New Addington. Hooks Joinery Works started between the wars in Ravenscroft Road before moving to Villiers where they are still operating. Smith & Haydn for many years had a sweet factory at Elmers End as did Henry Flack's the varnish manufacturers. Sisley's, the home-made sweet shop, was next to Sainsbury's. It was part of a small chain store based in London.

The list is endless and we regret having to omit so many. Look down all the alley ways between shops and you will be surprised at the number of small businesses there are in the district. Before ending this chapter we would like to mention the 'traders' we think of so nostalgically these days. The cats' meat man with his tray of skewered pieces, the muffin man with his hand bell, the 'stop me and buy one' Wall's ice cream man. Wall's had a factory in Avenue Road and just round the corner in Ravenscroft Road was the Eldorado depot. Besides deliveries of milk there were the travelling greengrocer and the daily baker. Paraffin was delivered to the door to say nothing of the coal carts and their patient horses. Last of all we should not forget the budding young entrepreneurs who would earn pocket money by collecting manure dropped by these horses to sell for 2d. a bucket to local gardeners. Some of these youngsters may well have gone on to start and run their own successful businesses.

Chapter VII

Beckenham at Prayer

Church of England, Non-Conformists, and Roman Catholic

In 1820, when the Langley property was put up for sale, Beckenham was described as a 'neighbourhood of the first respectability, and its situation particularly desirable for a nobleman or gentleman fond of hunting or shooting'. But was the situation equally delectable for the ploughman and cottagers upon the Beckenham landowners' estates? Did the church concern itself with their welfare? The old workhouse, for example (as we have seen in Chapter III), was not a 'particularly desirable' residence for its 24 inmates.

In 1861 the population of the village was 2,391 and 30 years later it was 20,707. A soaring population meant expanding spiritual requirements, and this in turn was reflected by a mushrooming of places of worship. Beckenham had only needed one church in the village, the parish church of St George. The earliest known rector is William de Knapton in 1294 and a list of his successors up to the present day will be found recorded just within the south door. In 1790

101. The old parish church of St George on the corner of Bromley Road and the High Street, *c*.1870. Its origins were probably in Saxon times and the building which served the needs of the small community until the late 19th century was based on a 14th-century structure.

102. The parish church of St George with an incomplete tower, c.1890. A choir vestry was added in 1890 but
the tower remained uncompleted for the next 13 years, the bells being hung in a temporary wooden shed on
the top of the unfinished tower during this period.

the old church was struck by lightning and partly destroyed by fire. It was 74 years before the
main building was restored and enlarged. The present building only dates from 1885-
87 during, which period the old church was demolished and the new one erected without the
services ever being interrupted. The earliest records at St George's date from 1538 when it
became compulsory for churches to keep records of all births, marriages and deaths in the
parish. These records were stored in a vault in the churchyard during the Second World War
as a protection against bomb damage, but they were badly attacked by damp.

As the Cator estate developed it became necessary to have more space for the extra
congregation and in 1864 St Paul's was built at New Beckenham.

The next church to be built was St Mary's, Shortlands, when the population for that area
was only two hundred and sixty. Shortlands was formed as a separate parish in 1870. The
original church was erected by the Wilkinson family of Shortlands House. The foundation
stone for the present church was laid in 1953, and the new building consecrated two years later
,but the traditional lych gate was not replaced.

In 1870 work was also begun on the first vicarage, situated on ground partly occupied by
the present church. This house, built by the local contractors, Syme & Duncan, was also
damaged beyond repair by enemy action and subsequently demolished. The vicarage was the
first dwelling to be completed by the then William Syme and John Duncan partnership. A
parish room had been built close by Shortlands station in 1882 and this was later enlarged and
went on to serve as the parish church after the bombing of 1940. The building was subsequently
sold in 1966 when the new church hall was opened in St Mary's Avenue.

Parish Church, Beckenham

103. St George's parish church soon after completion in 1903. Externally it looks much the same today.

104. The lych gate at St George's dates from the 13th century and is one of the oldest in the country. It was renovated in 1924 in memory of Stanley and Hedley Thornton who were killed in the First World War.

15579 ST. PAULS CHURCH.   BECKENHAM.

105. St Paul's church, at New Beckenham, *c.*1905. The first part
of the church opened in 1872 and a separate parish was created
when the main church with pews for 1,000 was consecrated.

106. St Mary's, Shortlands. The church and fine lych gate were
badly damaged by a landmine in 1940, and totally destroyed by a
doodlebug four years later.

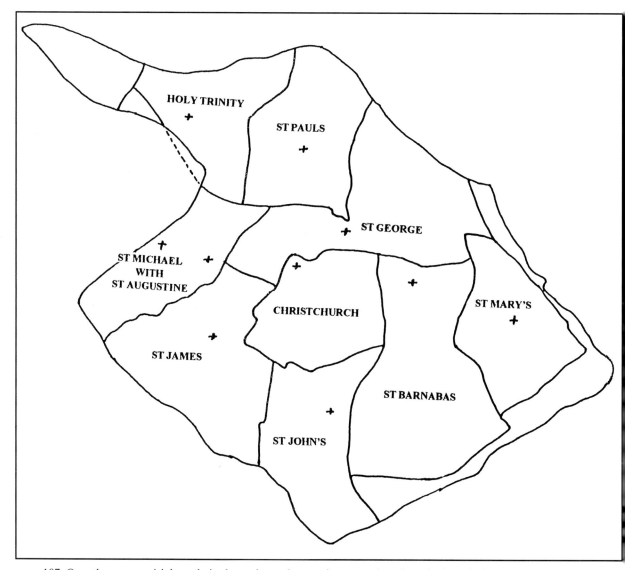

107. Over the years parish boundaries have changed many times; we show here the boundaries as they are today.

The last rector of St George's to preside over the undivided parish and a vestry which had the sole power over local affairs, both ecclesiastical and civil, was the Rev. Frederick Chalmers. He came to the parish in 1849, having previously had a very successful career as an officer in the Indian Army. With him came his father-in-law, Dr. Marsh, (also a clergyman) and his sister-in-law Catherine who probably became even better known than the two men for her evangelistic activities and prowess as the author of several books. Between them they made a formidable team, preaching the gospel to the numerous navvies who had come to the area for building both the railways and the Crystal Palace.

In 1873, to help reduce the pressure on accommodation in the parish church, a small corrugated iron chapel was erected in The Avenue, and William Welsh, a friend of the Rector's, was invited to take charge. The new chapel was called Christ Church. William Welch was a staunch evangelical. He wore a black Genevan gown and refused to wear a surplice until requested to do so by the Archbishop of Canterbury. Unfortunately, in the same year that Welch arrived, Frederick Chalmers,

108. The Rev. Frederick Chalmers rector of Beckenham from 1851-73 was a good organiser. During his stay the steeple was repaired, a hot water heating system installed, the old fashioned square pews in the chancel and nave were removed, the graveyard extended and the present stone wall erected in place of the old wooden palings.

who was then 68, decided to take up a quieter living at Nonington near Aylesham where he died 12 years later. Albemarle Cator, the Lord of the Manor, nominated his brother William, an Oxford graduate and high churchman, to succeed to the living. It is difficult today to appreciate the strength of feeling which differences in doctrine aroused amongst churchgoers in Victorian times. In 1877 many policemen were required to quell a riot at a church and the clergyman concerned was tried and sentenced to imprisonment for his Anglo-Catholic practices. Feelings also ran high in Beckenham, and as a result the congregation of Christ Church swelled from 45 to its capacity of 450 within a year.

When the Rev. William Cator came as Rector to St George's he found a church closed except on Sundays, infrequent celebrations of the Holy Communion, church doctrine of the lowest type, and church life apparently almost dead. The simple worship to which the community had been accustomed was changed and, during the first part of 1874, 'ultra ritualistic and ultra sacramental novelties—including the confessional—were introduced' into the parish church. It became again a stronghold of the Anglo-Catholic movement, causing serious divisions in the parish.

109. Christ Church, Fairfield Road. This picture taken in 1902 shows the barrier which made the lower part of Fairfield Road a cul-de-sac for many years.

In order to meet the need for a larger place of worship than the tin hut in The Avenue, and also to provide for the wants of the large evangelical section of the parish, Mr. Cornelius Lea Wilson, known as the Squire of Beckenham, generously gave a site in The Fairfield for the erection of a permanent church and vicarage, with Schoolhouse, Lecture Hall and Institute, together with a donation of £2,500 towards the Building Fund.

At first the new Rector of Beckenham (Rev. W. Cator) was very favourably disposed towards the erection of the new church, but before many months had passed his views underwent a complete change. The differences in doctrine and the realisation of the threat to his parish and income arising from the appearance of new and more splendid churches, built to serve the rapidly developing town, soured relations and from that time onward he persistently opposed every step connected with the establishment of the new church. However, the new scheme had advanced so far that his change of attitude did not affect the execution of the approved plans. The new Christ Church was consecrated by His Grace the Archbishop of Canterbury on 20 May 1876. The first incumbent was the Rev. William Welch, who had ministered in the temporary church in The Avenue. The old iron building was sold in 1877 and the money was used towards the debt on the lower school building. The church was severely damaged by a flying bomb during a raid in 1945 and not fully repaired until 1950.

There had been for many years a chapel attached to Kelsey Manor called St Agatha's Chapel and in July 1871 the annual festival of the English Church Union was held there.

The parish of St Barnabas was formed in 1877 and a temporary building went up in Oakhill Road. The following year the building of the church was started. It was done in stages, the whole not being completed until 1933. Like many other churches the building was badly damaged by bombs in 1944, but restored in 1948. In 1954 St Peter's Church Hall was built in Malmains Way to serve the Park Langley area and this has since been extended.

The building of Holy Trinity in Lennard Road in 1878 created another parish. The church was founded by Francis Peek, who was a tea merchant, and nephew of the founder of Peek, Frean and Company, the biscuit firm, and son of the founder of a tea firm called Peek Brothers. In 1876 his attention had been drawn to the growing needs of the poor neighbourhood which

110. St Michael's & All Angels on the Birkbeck estate, *c.*1918. In 1908 the district was made a parish with Fr. Armstrong as the first Vicar. St Michael's is very 'High Church' with incense, genuflecting, and confessionals.

was springing up on the edges of the Cator Estate at Beckenham. Owing to some provision that the class of property must not be beneath a certain value on this estate, the work people crowded to the border, and there must have been about this time a population of several thousands at Penge. For some years the spiritual needs of these folk had been provided by a school-room service in Penge Lane, and it was here that Francis Peek saw his opportunity. He gained the sympathy of Albemarle Cator, who gave the site, part of a field adjoining the Alexandra cottages. The first vicar was the Rev. S. Whitfield Daukes, who was then a curate at St Bartholomew's, Sydenham, and who married Mr. Peek's eldest daughter, Lydia. The church was opened in 1878. The church house opposite was once an exclusive boys' school run by the Rev. Whitfield Daukes. This building was demolished and the site redeveloped as housing in the mid-1980s.

From 1868 until 1877 St Michael's church was a little tin hall in Harding's Lane, in the Alexandra district of Beckenham. When Holy Trinity, Lennard Road, was built, St Michael's moved to the Birkbeck Estate, and another hut was put up in Birkbeck Road in 1877, but it was not until 1898 that the building of the new church, which was to face Ravenscroft Road, was started and it was another 37 years before it was completed.

Until 1879 the little hamlet known as 'the Elmers End District' consisted of a few hundred people only. The area was served by a small iron church in the Upper Elmers End Road opposite Goddard Road, but in February of that year a plot of land in Elmers End was given as a site for a church in a more accessible spot. By the end of that year the church was completed and the school was opened the following year. It was not until 1924 that St James' became a separate parish, the largest in Beckenham, and at that time, on the instruction of the Bishop of Rochester, the work, organisations and possessions associated with All Saints, Chaffinch Road, were transferred to St James. The Rev. C. J. Ritson who had been at All Saints took over the new parish of St James and remained there until his death in 1941. The church was badly damaged during the Second World War, but this did not stop any of the services. One of the authors (NT) recalls a war-time winter wedding there when everyone, including the bride and the vicar, had to wear top coats because there was no heating at all and the wind blew strongly through the broken windows.

1871 saw the erection of the Arthur Road Mission (now Churchfields Road). It was non sectarian, and evangelistic meetings were regularly held. Five years later the old Beckenham Mission was built in 1876 near Oakhill, Bromley Road. In 1937 the building was converted into flats and named 'Oakhill Court'.

With the continued growth in population, the Nonconformist churches began to be established. Methodism began in the 1830s and according to a Deptford circuit plan, services were held on Sundays. Methodist beginnings in Beckenham appear to be somewhat vague, but originally local preachers from Bromley held meetings in houses and the public hall was used for services. In the second half of the 19th century class distinctions were still clearly identifiable and many houses in Beckenham were very much 'upstairs-downstairs'. The rising middle classes, prospering in commerce and trade, were making their homes in this area. Broadly speaking, the 'top people' worshipped in established churches, whereas the Nonconformist churches drew upon the new middle classes and their workers and people engaged in service. Thus the scene was set for the birth of a new Wesleyan church in this developing area. Mr. Tom Copeland, father of Rob Copeland the historian, recalled that in the late 1870s he could remember 'Cottage Meetings' being held in his father's house on Sunday evenings about once a month. The first congregational services in Beckenham were started in 1877 by a group of people in an iron room at New Beckenham station.

111. Bromley Road Methodist church, *c.*1907. The church on the corner of Bevington Road was not too badly damaged during the Second World War, although it frequently lost windows and slates. The manse, however, was bombed and rendered uninhabitable. In the 1970s it was discovered that the spire was eroding and it was decided to remove it for safety.

Bromley Road, Beckenham.

The foundation of Beckenham Congregational church in Crescent Road dates from 1878, when a small band of people, then known as 'Dissenters', decided to worship together. They met in what later became the Church Hall. This was destroyed by bombing in 1941 when the church keeper was killed, and rebuilt in 1950. Elmers End Free church was an off-shoot of Anerley Congregational Church, beginning as a mission in 1869. In 1872 an iron hut was erected in Eden Road and five years later this was moved to Ancaster Road but later moved again to a free-hold site in Langley Road. In 1884 a brick building was erected adjoining it, and this became the daughter church of Beckenham Congregational church. Shortly after 1900 it was made self supporting. An agreement was made that no other Free Church should be built in the area, which is why it is still called 'Free', although it is in fact affiliated to the Congregational Union. The present church in Goddard Road was opened in 1931—the two previous buildings being used as halls. By this time many more people had moved to

112. Elm Road Baptist church, c.1912. In the early days of its history part of the church was screened off because the congregation was not big enough to fill it. It escaped serious damage during the Second World War but suffered a fire in 1950.

the new estates in the Elmers End and Eden Park areas. The Congregational church in Goddard Road was built in 1887.

Elm Road Baptist church was formally opened in 1883. It was built on the corner of Elm Road before any of the houses were erected. The London Baptist Association at that time had a policy of building one new church each year.

St Augustine's Mission Hall, Churchfields Road (formerly Arthur Road) opened in 1886, and in 1910 a dual purpose hall and church was started. This church was dedicated by the Bishop of Rochester on 1 July 1933 and consecrated on 31 May 1945. The Congregational church was started in Crescent Road, off Bromley Road and opened on 20 June 1888. In the same year a Wesleyan (Methodist) church was built in Bromley Road. The mission hall, known as the Lea Wilson Hall, stood in the High Street below Village Place until it was demolished in the 1920s when the High Street was widened. Another mission hall was built in Avenue Road, and the Ebenezer Baptist church at Elmers End near St Margaret's Villas in Croydon Road.

A mission hall had been built in Croydon Road, between the cottage hospital and Shaftesbury Road. This functioned under the auspices of Christ Church, and it was the worshippers from here who formed the nucleus of the congregation for the new church of St John's at Eden Park.

113. Croydon Road Mission Hall. The iron hut of the mission was transported to Eden Park Avenue and used for worship until the present St John's church was built in 1936.

St John's is an Anglican church, with no incense, and the congregation worship simply. The Eden Park area had been in the parish of St James', Elmers End and during 1930 delicate but friendly negotiations had gone on. In an age when differences of churchmanship were a much more passionate issue than they have mercifully become today, there were strong feelings that there should be an evangelical presence in the developing areas of South Beckenham. St James' to the west, and St Barnabas' to the east, were there for those who preferred 'high' services. Something was needed for those who valued simplicity of worship and an emphasis on Bible teaching. The parish boundaries between Christ Church and St James' were redrawn and the new area became a separate parish of St John the Baptist, with an evangelical tradition.

The church was damaged several times during the war losing windows and tiles, but it was not until just three months before the end of hostilities that it received its greatest blow. This was on 21 February 1945 when a V2 rocket landed causing grievous damage. The church itself lost all windows and half of the doors and the east wall was cracked away from the main structure. It was shored up temporarily but eventually had to be rebuilt. The organ loft was severely damaged and needed rebuilding and the vestries were virtually destroyed.

In 1907 two small churches were opened at Clock House. All Saints, which stood at the junction of Clock House Bridge and Chaffinch Road, was a mission church of St Augustine's and closed when St Augustine's was created a separate parish. The other was the Wesleyan Chapel in Clock House Road. This had been built as The Beckenham High School in 1895 but the opening of the Beckenham Technical Institute killed off the High School. For a few years it became a not very successful dance-cum-vaudeville hall before being rented by the Wesleyans, who finally bought it outright in 1909. The rooms used below ground by the Sunday school were once the theatre's dressing rooms.

The parish church was originally a Catholic church but from 1559, the year of the Reformation, until 1891 there was no Catholic parish nor Catholic rector in Beckenham. The worship of the Catholic religion was ruthlessly suppressed by the state, in Beckenham and throughout England, and the celebration of Holy Mass was made a penal offence punishable by death. The old parish church of St George, therefore, fell into Protestant hands, and both it and its successor have been used for the worship of the state church ever since. Before the Reformation, Beckenham was in the Catholic diocese of Rochester and the province of

Canterbury, and had been so since Pope St Gregory the Great appointed St Augustine first Archbishop of Canterbury in A.D. 597, and St Justus first Bishop of Rochester. Far earlier than this England had been ruled by Catholic bishops in communion with the Holy See of Rome. On the restoration of the Catholic hierarchy in England in 1851, the Catholic prelates were forbidden by the state to resume their ancient titles, and Beckenham is now, therefore, in the Catholic diocese of Southwark and Province of Westminster. The Catholic parish of Beckenham was re-instated in 1891, and its first post-Reformation rector was the Right Rev. W. H. Kirwan, who later became domestic Prelate to His Holiness the Pope.

By 1891 the first Roman Catholic church, the church of the Transfiguration and St Benedict was built in Overbury Avenue. The growth of Beckenham during the inter-war years made it increasingly necessary to have a more central place of worship, so in 1926 the church bought a hut in Village Way, which had formerly been erected as a United Services Club by the Y.M.C.A. in the First World War. The hut had become derelict so Father Pooley, the parish priest, and members of the congregation refurbished it to serve as a Catholic church, and this did yeoman service for many years. But the congregation was still growing and the hall became inadequate. In 1937 the foundation stone was laid for St Edmund's Church—46 years after the Catholic mission was begun in Beckenham.

A small chapel stood for a few years in Beckenham Road between Birkbeck Road and Mackenzie Road on the site now occupied by Northam's shop in Beckenham Road. Two other churches complete the picture in Beckenham, the Evangelical church at The Hall in Cromwell Road, and the Christian Witness Church in Rectory Road.

During the 19th and early 20th centuries many mothers would go to be 'Churched' after the birth of a baby, and babies were not thought to thrive until they had been baptised. Youngsters were often confirmed when only ten or eleven years old, if they were leaving home to find work or go into service. Customs have changed drastically since the Second World War.

114. St Benedict's Roman Catholic Church. The Church of the Transfiguration and St Benedict served the Catholics for many years, but it was rather out of the way in Overbury Avenue, which is one of the reasons why the new church was built in Village Way.

Chapter VIII

Beckenham at Leisure

Sports and Pastimes

The earliest leisure activities enjoyed by the residents of Beckenham were naturally of a rural nature. Cricket was played by the villagers on the Fair Field and there were private cricket grounds both at Beckenham Place and Kelsey. The Fair Field took its name from an annual fair which was held there each August until the 1850s. It was not ideal for cricket as the level area was limited and the field was crossed by two footpaths. It was not perhaps as inconvenient as it would be today, for in those days there were no boundaries and sides did not have to declare. Sometimes the fielding side did not have an opportunity to bat before bad light forced them to retire. Horse racing on the farm land between Croydon and Beckenham Roads was also a feature of the first half of the 19th century, until the Woodside racecourse opened beyond the Croydon boundary in 1866.

Organised sport dates from March 1866 when a group of enthusiasts led by Arthur Whaten of Beckenham Lodge met to found the Beckenham Cricket Club. They moved with remarkable speed: within two months they had leased the Beckenham Place ground at Foxgrove, held their first dinner at *The Three Tuns* with Peter Cator in the chair, and played their first match.

115. Foxgrove cricket pavilion. The club has continued to play on its original ground until the present day and includes Dr. W. G. Grace among its famous visitors. The first county fixture—Kent v. Surrey—was played there in 1886.

116. Cricket at the Crystal Palace. Foxgrove was by no means the only cricket ground in Beckenham. The London County Cricket Club, of which Dr. W.G. Grace was Secretary and Manager from 1899 to 1908, had its home pitch in the grounds of Crystal Palace within the Beckenham boundary.

Tennis was introduced in 1879 at Foxgrove and two years later ladies were permitted to join. The sport became so popular that in 1886 an annual open tournament was introduced, which over the years has attracted most of the famous players to Beckenham. Today the week-long Lawn Tennis Tournament and Kent All-comers Championships serve as a prelude to Wimbledon and attract an entry of international tennis stars to Beckenham every June.

Two sports arenas were built at the Crystal Palace, straddling the Penge/Beckenham boundary. Here were played the first cup finals, and they became the scene of motor, motor bike and cycle racing. This complex was replaced by the National Sports Centre so, whilst the competitors involved came from all parts of the country, Beckenham can rightly feel that it has been and still is the scene of sporting endeavour from the most humble to that of the greatest national significance.

117. The tennis club in Albemarle Road, c.1913. The club was the first to welcome competitors from the Soviet Union and the first to attract commercial sponsorship.

The town is also the home of the national sports grounds of three of the High Street banks and of a number of other large commercial concerns. New Beckenham was the nearest place to the city where cheap flat land with a good train service was available.

The Beckenham Men's Swimming Club was founded in 1879, but it did not have local facilities until the baths were opened in 1901 on the site of the old Clock House. It had both covered and open air pools.

The original baths had no facilities for women bathers and the Ladies' Swimming Club was not formed until 1921. Beckenham swimmers have always been able to field strong teams in national and international competitions and several members of both clubs have represented Britain in the Olympics. The men's water polo team has been considered to be one of the finest in the country.

There was an ever-growing need to cater for schoolchildren once swimming became a compulsory school subject. However it was 1938 before funds became available for the baths to be completely redesigned and up-dated.

There were no public parks nor recreation grounds, and the loss of the Fair Field for a church and housing in the 1870s deprived the villagers of their traditional open space. Whilst Beckenham was surrounded by open fields this was not too much of a handicap. The rector frequently permitted his paddock in Rectory Road to be used for local sporting activities.

In 1890 the Local Board purchased a meadow in Croydon Road next to the cottage hospital for a recreation ground. It was formally opened the following year when the gentry, clergy, tradespeople and representatives of every organisation and all the schoolchildren, each wearing a medal specially minted for the occasion, made their way through the flag-bedecked village with bands playing and church bells ringing.

118. As can be seen from the picture, c.1928, the layout of the park has not greatly changed up to the present day. Hospital Meadow was added in 1914 and survived an attempt at compulsory purchase for hospital extension in 1953. Access to Village Way was created in the 1930s.

119. The ornamental lake in Croydon Road Recreation Ground, *c*.1915. Its fountain, which came from the Clock House grounds, was replaced by the present paddling pool just before the war.

Alexandra Park was also opened in 1891, seemingly without ceremony. In 1907 a two-acre site belonging to the Churchfields Charity was purchased by the council as a recreation ground for the Birkbeck area. A condition of the sale was that the name Churchfields Recreation Ground should be used to perpetuate the memory of its source.

The opening of the recreation grounds signalled an explosion of sporting activity. The annual cricket match between the coachmen and gardeners of the local gentry became an important annual event. Cricket was by no means the only sport popular in the area. Bowls at Croydon Road commenced as early as 1902 and the West Beckenham Bowling Club at the Alexandra ground was founded in 1919.

Football has always been popular, and many churches and schools fielded teams. The Beckenham & District League dates from 1912. Rugby has had a more chequered career. There was a Beckenham Rugby Club in 1876 but the present club commenced in 1894 though it was moribund from 1914 until 1924, and did not acquire its present site, a former polo ground, until a year or two later.

Beckenham has had four golf clubs, though only two still remain. The oldest, Beckenham Golf Club, opened in 1891, on the site of the former Woodside race course, and closed towards the end of the last war. The ladies formed their own club at Shortlands in 1894 to which men had only restricted access. In 1907 the Foxgrove Golf Club leased ground in Beckenham Place Park, but lost its greens to the public in 1928, though the club house still remains. The last to be formed was Park Langley Club in 1910, the brainchild of the estate's developers.

Angling was at one time allowed in the lake at Kelsey Park and for many years there has been a very active club using the small lake in the Crystal Palace grounds, whilst the lower boating lake is open to all for fishing.

120. Bowls in Beckenham Recreation Ground, *c*.1906. A game of bowls being played in the early days of this century. A much larger jack (the white ball) was then used and the rink had a white line or tape down the centre.

121. Holy Trinity Football Team 1905-6. Most schools and churches had their own enthusiastic football club. Apart from their long shorts, the kit is little different from today's wear.

122. Golf at Beckenham Place Park. Golf has been played in the park since 1907, first under the auspices of the Foxgrove Golf Club and since 1928 on a public course.

123. Crystal Palace Angling Club's pavilion, c.1959. Sadly the pavilion was burnt down some years ago by vandals.

Perhaps the biggest event to be staged was the annual flower show. The Alexandra estate tenants had formed the Alexandra District Floral and Horticultural Society in 1868 and held annual shows from that date. At their first event over 300 money and special prizes were awarded. Beckenham Horticultural Society was formed in 1892 and proceeded to mount annual shows which rivalled Chelsea. There were dozens of large gardens in the town each with extensive glass houses run by several gardeners. The incentive to outdo your neighbour was intense and the resulting spectacle something we shall never see again.

In addition to the annual flower show, Croydon Road recreation ground has been the scene of almost every civic and national occasion the town has celebrated. The shallow oval depression near the entrance, sometimes referred to as the Hippodrome, was flooded in winter and used as a skating rink. The same site was the scene of a unique occasion in 1902 when, to celebrate the coronation of King Edward VII, Britain's first public mail, carrying balloon soared aloft with M. Gaudron, a French balloonist and Dr. Barton, a local medical practitioner, as crew. Mail was dropped at three points in Kent and the balloon itself then crossed the Channel and landed near Calais. Two more balloons ascended from the same spot at the 1905 flower show and, although by this time airmail had lost its novelty, the few cards which have survived are eagerly sought by collectors.

124. Fishing for tiddlers in Cator Park. Youngsters have always enjoyed 'tiddler fishing', although now the local streams have been culverted to reduce flooding there are few places left for them to be able to enjoy this simple pleasure.

125. Beckenham Flower Show, c.1910. Support started to dwindle after the First World War and the society finally collapsed in the 1970s—though its Floral Art Section has survived to this day as a separate organisation.

Although the annual Flower Show and the Hospital Fête together with its traditional fair are no longer held, the crowning of the Beckenham May Queen still takes place on the first Saturday in April every year, following a procession through the district of all the May Queens and their attendants from West Wickham, Eden Park, Penge, Anerley, and Hayes.

Perhaps the proudest occasion the recreation ground was to witness was in 1935 when the Lord Mayor of London drove into the park in his ceremonial coach to present a Charter of Incorporation as a borough on behalf of H.M. The King.

A proposal to purchase the whole of the manor estate for the town was rejected but fortunately a later one to acquire the Kelsey grounds was successful. It had been realised that there was a need for an ornamental park as distinct from a recreation ground. Kelsey manor was demolished in 1921, the site sold for housing and the proceeds used to improve access and acquire the extension fronting onto Wickham Road which was opened in 1936.

Between the wars the town pursued a generous policy of acquiring additional recreational space for its residents. Cator Park, formerly a private park called the Kent House Pleasure Ground, was acquired, as were the Stanhope playing fields. The site of Eden Farm was bought by the local council early this century when the house was demolished and later Crease Park, facing on to Village Way, was created and named after Alderman James Crease who was the second Charter Mayor and one of the five freemen of the borough.

126. Thornton's shop decorated for the Coronation in 1902. Three hundred cards were overprinted 'BECKENHAM CELEBRATION. Despatched from the Clouds by Balloon Post, Coronation Day, Aug. 9th 1902'. The cards were sold for 3d. each and were to be addressed and stamped, with a written message if desired, and then left at Thornton's library. The cards were quickly sold out.

Despatched from the Clouds by
Balloon Post,
Coronation Day,
Aug. 9th, 1902.

"LONG MAY THEY REIGN."

BECKENHAM
CELEBRATION.

KING EDWARD VII.
BORN NOV 9, 1841

QUEEN ALEXANDRA.
BORN DEC 1, 1844

MARRIED MARCH 10, 1863
ACCESSION JANUARY 22, 1901

127. Front of a balloon card. Today only about half a dozen of the 1902 Coronation balloon cards are known to exist. Airmail collectors covet them because they were the first mail ever to be flown in a manned balloon. At an auction in 1980 one of these cards fetched £1,500.

128. The back of a balloon card. The postmark on this card is 'Dover, 4 November 1902'. The delay was due to the fact that one of the sacks of mail landed in a field and was undiscovered for three months.

POST CARD

129. Elgood playing fields; a march past and salute at the opening of the fields in 1928. Hitler had not yet come to power and the raised arm salute did not have its later significance.

The school children had not been forgotten and in 1928 the Elgood playing fields were opened between Village Way and Manor Way. The local elementary school children of all ages walked there for their weekly games and for the annual inter-school sports which were one of the highlights of the scholastic year. Another equally important event was the inter-school gala when the first-class baths rang with the deafening roars of encouragement from the gallery and water-side.

Whilst catering for a wide range of sporting activities, Beckenham at first lacked public facilities for cultural interests. In 1882 a Public Hall Co. was formed to purchase part of the site of the old manor house from the local board and to build and operate a hall on the site. Opening in 1884, it was immediately in great demand. Most of the ground floor was leased to a gentlemen's club which still exists in part of the building almost unchanged to this day. The public hall still largely retains its original appearance. It remained the property of the private company until after the war when it was purchased by Beckenham Council.

In 1897 Church House was opened in the gardens of the old rectory fronting on to the High Street. This was much used by church organisations and other societies. The Photographic and Cine societies were both founded in its committee rooms and the horticultural society used it not only to hold meetings but also to house its considerable library of over 500 volumes. Before the advent of wireless and television, people had to arrange their own entertainment and clubs and societies of every sort were well supported. The founding in 1883 of a College of Music and Art in Rectory Road which advertised a staff of no less than 50 professors, and the opening of the public hall the following year, sparked off a flurry of musical activity. The Beckenham Orchestral Society was founded in 1883, the Choral Society in 1885, and the Amateur Dramatic Club five years later. Round about 1890 the Beckenham Brass Band was formed and practised at *The George*, which was also the home of an indoor bowls club. The outbreak of war sounded the death knell of most of these organisations for, just as today, they depended in large measure on the efforts and enthusiasm of relatively few individuals, many of whom did not return from the fighting. Between the wars some societies, such as the Amateur Dramatic Society, reformed. A Beckenham Society, the forerunner of the present Civic Society, also made its appearance between the wars.

130. The Pavilion cinema on the corner of Village Way, in the 1920s. There are still people in Beckenham today who can recall the old silent films, the tinkling piano and the lady who threaded your token on a string when you entered. Even the new-fangled tip-up seats were a great novelty and sometimes a snare to the uninitiated.

131. The Odeon cinema at Elmers End, in the 1950s. This cinema opened just as the Second World War commenced, but only survived for 18 years before competition from television took its toll.

This was also the heyday of the picture palace. Beckenham's first cinema, the Pavilion, opened in October 1914 with a programme of patriotic war films and all proceeds were donated to the town's war relief fund. It did not long survive the Regal which opened in 1930 and is still with us today as the Cannon. Typically, it provided an escape from humdrum reality with fitted carpets, soft lighting and luxurious fittings not yet standard in the average home. Before the film started the lights would dim and the organist would slowly rise from the pit, playing his mighty Wurlitzer ablaze with light. The Regal cinema had a seating capacity of 1,980 and opened on 22 September 1930 with 'The Rogue Song'. The Odeon at Elmers End opened on 26 August 1939 with 'The Man In The Iron Mask'. It had a seating capacity of 1,518 but, due to the popularity of television in the 1950s, it closed in January 1957 when the site was demolished and redeveloped with Muirheads office tower. Its last screening was 'Dance With Me Henry' and 'Overland Pacific'.

A public library, opened in 1939, was one amenity Beckenham was surprisingly late in acquiring. Subscription libraries were run by Boots, Smiths and Thorntons, so the council presumably felt this was adequate until the growth of the suburban estates in the town centre and along Croydon Road.

Chapter IX

Beckenham at War

1914-1918 and 1939-1945

Beckenham has never been found wanting in times of war. On 22 April 1798, 63 residents gathered on the Fair Field and resolved to form an Armed Association to defend the country against the French under Napoleon should the need arise, but their services were not required. In the second half of the 19th century military cadets were a commonplace sight in the town. The East India Company's Military Training College was situated at nearby Addiscombe and its trainees were encouraged to visit the town by Frederick Chalmers, Rector of Beckenham from 1850 to 1873, himself an ex-Indian Army man. In 1900, during the Boer War, a Volunteer Corps was formed and had its headquarters at Elm Cottage in the High Street.

Not everyone considered that it was patriotic to give up one's job to serve the country. One volunteer, returning after fighting in the Boer War, was given a reference which read: 'This young man had so little consideration for his employer and his own prospects that he abandoned his job to fight in South Africa'.

The First World War had a drastic effect on the town. The cream of its manhood enrolled in the armed forces, many of them never to return. A number of the larger buildings became military headquarters or hospitals to take care of the wounded. Christ Church Halls and Balgowan Schools, for example, became military hospitals, the former only until 1916 when the operation was moved to the newly-built Lennard Road Girls County School. This 130-bed establishment had an operating theatre, X-Ray and the latest electrical apparatus. It closed on the last day of 1918.

Throughout the county Red Cross detachments, St John's Ambulance Brigade and territorial forces had been preparing since 1912 in case of emergency. The Beckenham Red Cross had been doing their training at the Cottage Hospital over the previous two years. Kent 86 Red Cross detachment took over the hasty preparation of the Christ Church Schools and converted the rooms into a hospital of 50 beds. Kent 96 detachment, aided by Kent 162, at first assisted Kent 86 at the Christ Church Schools site but they were then transferred to the new school building in Balgowan Road. Like Lennard Road this was fully equipped with the latest technology and had 100 beds to start with, but the addition of two marquees enabled the accommodation to be increased to 240 beds. The hospital closed on 31 March 1919 and both schools shortly after were returned to the education board.

When one considers the vast numbers treated at these two hospitals alone, it brings home to us how many thousand personnel were injured during the First World War, to say nothing about the numbers who did not survive to be sent home. Beckenham is the only place we are recording here, but it must be appreciated that numerous other towns in the country can tell the same tale. Two thousand wounded arrived at Bromley South station on the first day that casualties were returned to Britain.

132. Christ Church Hospital in 1915. This Red Cross hospital, together with the annexe at Kelsey Cottage, was closed and transferred to the new building in Lennard Road in 1916 but the name Christ Church Hospital was retained.

133. Balgowan School Military Hospital in Balgowan Road, *c*.1917. The hospital admitted 5,257 soldiers and a further very large number attended as out-patients.

134. Funeral of a Belgian soldier in Fairfield Road in 1915. Many of the casualties did not survive and, like this Belgian soldier, were buried with full military honours at Elmers End cemetery.

135. Oakwood at Shortlands, seen here in 1915, was taken over by one of the military transport divisions.

136. The Y.M.C.A. canteen, c.1917. To satisfy the social needs of the military visitors, the Y.M.C.A. erected a large hut as a services club in the cul-de-sac by the side of the Pavilion cinema.

137. Beckenham's Peace Parade in 1919. Everyone turned out to celebrate and enjoy the Peace Parade as it wound its way from the parish church through the village High Street. Every organisation which had been connected with the war effort took part.

138. Like so many of the large houses in Beckenham, Village Place in the High Street became a military establishment for the duration.

139. War memorials of all sizes were erected in every town and village throughout Britain. This one, seen here in the 1920s, was near St Mary's church at Shortlands.

Besides the wounded personnel, the village was host to several battalions of soldiers, English, Scottish, Irish and Canadian who were billeted throughout the district wherever anyone had a spare bed. Men in khaki were an all too familiar sight and so were those in hospital blue. Beckenham also became home for the many Belgian refugees within a month of the commencement of hostilities, and their children went to Bromley Road school. In a matter of weeks village life changed drastically, never to return quite the same after the armistice. The first Belgians to arrive were 36 trades people who had lost their all and been compelled to leave their country. Two large houses, one at the junction of Manor Road and Wickham Road, and one at Shortlands were equipped with all the necessary furniture and bedding etc. Two more houses and a clothing depot were quickly organised.

Many of the large buildings affected by their military occupation were never again to be family homes and were eventually demolished. When peace came Beckenham was a very different place. Between the wars the memory of the carnage remained vivid among those who survived. One in ten of our men died. 11 November, Armistice Day, with its two minutes' silence was solemnly observed each year. Memorials were erected in prominent positions at the end of the High Street and outside St Mary's Shortlands. A new extension was added to the Cottage Hospital in memory of those who gave their lives. The lych gate outside St George's parish church was restored in memory of Hedley and Stanley Thornton, two of the sons of the town's newspaper proprietor who were killed in the conflict. The British Legion had strong local support with headquarters first in the Y.M.C.A. hut and later in the Manor House in the High Street.

140. Only two decades after the signing of the Armistice it was necessary once again to prepare for a further conflict. This 1941 photograph shows the newly formed Home Guard being inspected in Beckenham Recreation Ground.

141. The funeral cortège of 19 Auxiliary Fire Service personnel killed in a blitz on the East End in April 1943.

The Second World War was to have a very different but equally drastic and more direct effect on the town. Parks, sports grounds and other open sites were dug up for allotments, often sharing the space with soldiers, anti-aircraft guns and barrage balloons. There was even a rail-mounted gun which was shunted out from its tunnel hideout on the Sanderstead line from time to time. Every able-bodied person not conscripted into the forces was involved in the war effort in one way or another. A.R.P. personnel, both male and female, were recruited for firewatching and other necessary duties, such as a census on the size of water tanks in houses which might be needed in an emergency. An auxiliary fire service was recruited and the Local Defence Volunteers, later named the Home Guard, absorbed not only the older men but also youngsters awaiting conscription into the armed forces. Initially only a few rifles were issued to the staff in the factories at Elmers End and at the borough electricity works but, as in the early part of the war there was a very real threat of an attack on London by German ground forces, detailed plans were drawn up for the defence of the borough and the capital in which the 1,000 strong 55th West Kent Battalion of the Home Guard had a key role to play. So important was this role that the local battalion was personally inspected soon after its formation by no less a person than H.M. The King.

At the start of the Second World War the whole country was plunged into darkness when all street lighting was switched off and windows were blacked out. People very quickly adapted to managing with torch light. However it was slightly different in the First World War. The Urban District Council were quickly asking, 'Is Beckenham Too Dark?'—and this when the street lighting was at first only reduced. It was then suggested that they be suppressed

142. Spitfire fund raising at Muirhead's in 1940. The Mayor of Beckenham poses in front of an aircraft to publicise the event.

143. In one of the worst incidents in the borough both sides of this area of Beckenham Road were devastated when a V1 hit Bill Trendall's crowded café at lunchtime on 2 August 1944, killing 44 people.

144. St George's parish church was extensively damaged in July 1944 when two flying bombs devastated the area. The nearby shops and houses were never rebuilt and the resultant open space is today a pleasant oasis.

completely but it was felt that in certain places this would be dangerous, such as the path under the railway at the Kingshall Road allotments. There were no really hard and fast rules about a blackout at first, and at the council meeting in mid-October 1918 it was reported that the Beckenham end of Venner Road was in darkness, but at the Sydenham end the lights were brighter than than they had ever been. Also, whilst Beckenham was in darkness, the Crystal Palace was a blaze of lights and could be seen for miles. Doubtless everywhere conformed to the regulations once the Zeppelin raids commenced.

Days before the Second World War actually started many thousands of schoolchildren and mothers with young children were evacuated from the large towns into more rural areas where it was felt they would be safer from air attacks. Many left on private schemes for Canada and the U.S.A. Beckenham did not really organise evacuation until the raids became so severe during the winter of 1940-41, and even then children had to live on the Penge side of the Clock House railway line. Thus if you lived in Sidney Road you were considered to be at risk but safe the other side of the railway in Clock House Road. However the whole area was soon to be at risk, as raids intensified and the rockets arrived.

A few evacuees never returned to Beckenham, preferring their new of life in the country, and many kept in touch with their foster families for many years. A small group of 21 girls left Lennard Road school early one dark and dismal morning in January 1941 and with their teacher spent the next 16 months in Exeter before several of them were bombed in the Exeter blitz of April 1942. One girl sadly lost her life in a bombing incident in Penge when she returned home, but of the rest half of them are still in touch with each other after 52 years and now have an annual reunion with Miss Rabson, who was their teacher in exile.

Schools were late opening for the autumn term 1939. Some forms only attended mornings or afternoons whilst other were taught in local houses. As the war progressed lessons often had to continue in the shelters but education, although interrupted for many, had to and did continue much as before. Allotments became highly desirable as food convoys were attacked by submarines. School playing fields and park land were dug up to provide more growing space. Girls at 18 years of age who did not want to join the armed services were able to go into the Land Army and help 'Dig for Britain' whilst the boys could opt to become Bevin Boys and go down the coal mines. For some years after the war boys were still being called up at 18 years of age to do a two-year National Service stint.

Ration books and gas masks were every day articles. One never went out at the beginning of the Second World War without carrying a gas mask in its little cardboard box. But as time went on they were left at home more and more often. Clothing coupons caused everyone to 'make do and mend' and an old parachute was highly prized for making undies. Wallpaper disappeared and rooms, needing to be redecorated, were painted with distemper. Some people turned vegetarian in order to get an increased cheese ration and many started to keep chickens in their back gardens to help out with the egg supplies. Pig clubs sprang up everywhere and nothing was allowed to be wasted. How things have changed since those days!

Beckenham was a legitimate target for air attack; not only did it lie on a main rail line to the capital, it also housed a large electronics factory as well as several smaller ones— even the Chinese Garage was on war work. It was also a convenient place to unload a bomb load should an aircraft be frustrated in reaching the centre of London. During the war nearly 1,000 high explosive bombs, 10,000 incendiaries and 79 V1 and V2 rockets rained down on the borough, killing 360 people and injuring almost 1,800 more.

Lord Stamp, Charter Mayor of Beckenham, was an early victim when his Shortlands home received a direct hit in April 1941. Two days later 21 Beckenham firemen perished in an

145. Incendiaries at St Michael's church. Sadly, within ten years of being finished, St Michael's and All Angels was completely destroyed by fire during an air raid on 24 March 1944, but was rebuilt and consecrated on 7 October 1956.

incident whilst on duty in the East End. The most conspicuous damage resulted from rocket attacks in July 1944 in which the Albemarle Road area and St Mary's church, Shortlands were both hit twice and Elmers End bus garage was totally destroyed. The worst loss of life came at the beginning of the following month when a crowded café in Beckenham Road was hit. In January 1945, just when everyone was beginning to think the worst was over, a V1 rocket wrecked Christ Church and the surrounding houses. This was the 73rd and last flying bomb to fall on the town, killing 12 people and seriously injuring several others. Although the church was badly damaged it was possible a few months later to hold a V.E. Day thanksgiving service amid the ruins.

Many awards for bravery were won during the wars both by military personnel and civilians. We mentioned in Chapter V Lt. John Norwood who earned the V.C. at Ladysmith. William Evans (Manchester Regt.) won the Victoria Cross at Guillemont, France in 1916. He was buried at Elmers End cemetery in 1937. Two more V.C.s connected with Beckenham were awarded during the Second World War. L/Cpl J. P. Harman (Royal West Kent Regt.) won his V.C. in April 1944 when the Japanese in Burma attempted to invade India. Lance Corporal John Harman was born in Beckenham and his medal was awarded posthumously. Captain P. J. Gardner (Royal Tank Regt.) received the Victoria Cross for his bravery during an attack by German tanks at Tobruk in November 1941. He had earlier received the M.C. Capt. Gardner was Chairman and Managing Director of J. Gardner & Co. Ltd., the steel fabrication company who built their factory on the site of the old Beckenham brick works.

Despite all this trauma and tragedy, a semblance of normal life went on both for the residents and their numerous military guests. Regular dances were held at the Regal and astronomical quantities of cups of tea and buns were consumed within the Christ Church Halls. British restaurants were also a regular feature of life at the St George's Church Hall in the High Street and at Muirheads. A Prisoner-of-War camp was in Beckenham and when peace came the prisoners helped to build the council houses in Beck Lane, near the Elmers End bus garage.

146. A wedding in the Church Hall. Whilst the church was being rebuilt all services were conducted in the Church Hall and in the case of weddings most photographs were taken in the vicarage grounds. This wedding was on 29 April 1950.

Many American and Canadian troops were stationed around the area and some married local girls and took them home as G.I. brides.

During the Second World War there was a campaign to encourage everyone to have holidays at home, and an outdoor stage was erected in the Croydon Road recreation ground on which entertainments were staged during the summer months. This action had not been necessary in the First World War as the majority of people then could not afford to go away on holiday.

Nearly a hundred and fifty years had lapsed between the villagers gathering in the Fair Field with their weapons and their descendants gathering in shelters to escape the devastation of pilotless aircraft. Truly Beckenham can be said to have experienced war in many of its aspects.

Chapter X

Postwar Beckenham

1945 to the Present Day

The years since the last war have witnessed change in Beckenham almost as radical as that which converted the original village into a town. Virtually every vestige of local control has passed either to regional or national authorities and Beckenham is now a dormitory suburb. This change did not come all at once and was due to a variety of reasons. Hospitals and electricity supply passed into outside hands due to political decisions made soon after war ended. Beckenham hospital at first benefited from the change with improved facilities but in recent years its future role has become uncertain. Its position was not helped by competition from the 30-bed Sloane Private Hospital which opened in Albemarle Road in 1980 and has since almost doubled in size. Control of the fire service was lost at the beginning of the war when it was realised that a vast increase in resources and a standardisation of equipment was essential to meet the threat posed by air attack. The fire station next to the public hall became redundant when a new combined fire and ambulance station was opened by the London Fire Brigade in Beckenham Road in 1985. The final blow, as far as Beckenham is concerned, came in 1965 when the borough was abolished and became part of a new London administrative unit called, rather confusingly, the London Borough of Bromley.

Perhaps the most drastic change to take place in the area stemmed from the gradual concentration of local government functions in Bromley once the borough had been abolished. The Town Hall stood derelict for a considerable time before being replaced by a Marks & Spencer food store in 1992. Fortunately its foundation stone, and that of the 18th-century rectory which had also stood on the site, were preserved and can now be seen in the parish church across the road..

The North Central Beckenham Redevelopment Scheme envisaged the complete replacement of the remaining shops and houses by an open space surrounded by modern office buildings. It succeeded inasmuch as Church Road was closed and Albemarle Road re-aligned to form the first stage of a proposed bypass for the town centre, thus creating the existing 'Beckenham

147. The 1963-4 council gathered in the Council Chamber for a formal photograph.

148. The headquarters of Beckenham Council and its predecessors from 1882 to 1932 being demolished in 1992 to make way for commercial redevelopment.

149. Beckenham Green. This small, peaceful area has been created out of the havoc caused by rockets which fell behind the church in 1944.

Green'. The church was more than willing to fit in with the council's plans, as even before the war it had regarded Church House as unsuited to modern requirements and something of a liability because of its state of repair. As a result, the church acquired the site of the old main post office in Albemarle Road on which to build a new hall, and Church House was demolished to be replaced by the present St Bride's House.

The nearby railway station has survived largely unchanged apart from slight modifications. The remains of what was built as Station Parade in the 1930s, but latterly was mainly occupied by Jones' timber merchants, was cleared in 1992. The main change has been the complete closure of the goods yard which within living memory was used to receive cattle on the hoof from Smithfield destined for a local butcher. Before the Clean Air Act in the 1960s Beckenham had often been reduced virtually to a standstill by the impenetrable fogs which occurred. But the Act, whilst removing the dangers of 'pea soupers', greatly reduced the urban coal market and the goods sidings at most of the smaller stations were closed and in many cases, as at Ravensbourne, the sites were used for commerce or housing. Much of the remaining local traffic was concentrated at Beckenham Junction, but even this dwindled due to competition from road transport resulting in ultimate closure. At the time of writing the yard lies partly derelict awaiting commercial redevelopment.

150. The centenary of the railway in 1956. This was commemorated by a steam-hauled excursion which is seen here leaving Beckenham Junction.

151. This early Tesco's supermarket is seen in 1968 during one of the periodic floods which used to affect this part of Beckenham whenever there was exceptionally heavy rain.

152. The interior of Beckenham's original Sainsbury's when it converted to self service in 1963.

Although the pattern of shops along the High Street has not basically changed, there are some trends worthy of mention. Many of the national chains of shops which were household names after the war such as Mac Fisheries, Montague Burtons, International Stores, Home & Colonial, have disappeared. Shop chains are now often franchised. Examples in Beckenham include Kall Kwik, Prontaprint, Pizza Hut, Wimpy. The house price boom resulted in a rash of estate agencies and estate agency mergers which saw the demise of some of the older firms such as Baxter, Payne & Lepper. This was followed by an invasion of charity shops. Building societies increased rapidly, especially after the banks ceased to open on Saturday mornings.

More significant has been the appearance of self service and the supermarket. Tesco set up in an existing shop but soon abandoned the experiment. Sainsbury's went over to self service in 1961 before finally closing in 1972. Finefare was the first purpose-built supermarket in the High Street. It survives to this day as Iceland after a period as Bejam, despite its lack of in-house parking facilities. It was succeeded by Safeway, much bigger and with considerable parking space at the rear. Later still Sainsbury's returned to the town after a lapse of 11 years with even greater sales space and parking facilities.

The rest of the High Street has undergone less drastic surgery apart from *The Greyhound* public house which was replaced in the '60s by the present modern office block whose public house ground floor was later re-named *The Beckenham*. At the other end of the High Street, the area round the War Memorial has changed little since 1939 when the post office was erected. The Regal cinema, now the Cannon, looks the same from the outside as when it was built. It was converted into three smaller cinemas in 1979 with:- Screen 1—587 seats; Screen 2—295 seats; and Screen 3—124 seats. Its Wurlitzer organ has survived and can still be heard in its new home, a private house in the Midlands.

It is not only the shopping streets which have undergone a transformation since the war. At the end of hostilities virtually the whole of the Cator estate, including some much used thoroughfares such as Albemarle Road, were unmade roads of the sort that can still be found at the top end of The Avenue and elsewhere. The Knoll, Plawsfield and Barnmead Roads are still unmade for their entire length—the latter was made a private road with restricted access. Not only have these roads been made up and their maintenance passed to the council but many large Victorian and Edwardian houses were demolished to make way for blocks of flats or small town houses. Bomb sites were rebuilt as office blocks, several of which have never been fully occupied, such as those on Beckenham Road at Mackenzie Road and Thayers Farm Road. Developments were not confined to the Cator estate; the value of land in the area had become so high that every piece of undeveloped land was sought by developers. In an imaginative deal the council traded land for housing at the rear of the swimming baths for a new leisure centre.

A limited number of special lace panels were made by Dobsons and M. Browne & Co. Ltd. of Nottingham. These were presented to Sir Winston Churchill, the Air Council, the Royal Air Forces Association, the City of London and to a limited number of towns including Beckenham, Croydon and Sheerness. The lace panels are 15 ft. high and ornately designed with scenes commemorating the war. The Beckenham panel was loaned to the Royal Air Force Station at Biggin Hill in 1970 for safekeeping and was displayed in the Officers' Mess. With the closure of the Station in 1992 the lace was then transferred to Bromley where, after refurbishment, it has been hung in the Civic Centre for all to see.

153. The Beckenham lace. The lace depicts badges and national flowers of the allied Air Forces, views of London, and various British and German aircraft.

154. The scene on the stage as the late Dick Emery declares the Beckenham Theatre Centre open in the presence of the Mayor and Mayoress of Beckenham, 24 September 1960. Victor Thornton can be seen sitting at the right of the picture.

By 1951 Beckenham had a population of 75,000 (10,000 more than Bromley), making it one of the largest towns in Kent. Local newspapers had for many years relied on the durability of old-fashioned equipment and the loyalty and enthusiasm of their founding families for their continued existence. Individually they did not generate the sort of profits required to invest in new technology, and as the years went by they became increasingly vulnerable to takeover by larger, better equipped organisations. Thus in 1955 control of the *Beckenham Journal* was sold to the *Kentish Times* who retained Victor Thornton as Editor until his death in 1966 but immediately closed the local printing works and transferred production to Sidcup. Since that date increasing commercial pressures have forced the closure of the local office, and whilst the name is still mentioned in the heading, the Beckenham content is minimal. The rival *Beckenham & Penge Advertiser* has fared little better, also closing its local office and quite recently abandoning the use of the title altogether.

Editor Victor Thornton joined others to persuade the council to close the High Street in order that a fair could be held to celebrate the Queen's coronation in 1953. And it was Victor Thornton who made his own contribution to the day by producing an open-air performance of *The Merry Wives of Windsor* in a replica Elizabethan playhouse beside the big tulip tree in Kelsey Park. It was thanks to Victor's father, Tom Thornton, that Kelsey Park was available for this performance. Tom had fought hard to convince the council that the Kelsey estate should be bought for use as a public park and it was due to his efforts that this was done and the park opened in 1913. Plans had already been drawn up to turn the estate into a housing complex when the council stepped in to buy it.

155. None of the participants on the stage in Victor Thornton's production of Shaw's masterpiece, *Pygmalion*, was over 15 years old. This show was performed at the Beckenham Baths in 1949.

As with the First World War, many societies which suspended their activities in 1939 did not revive after the war. The Cine Society was a casualty but one postwar venture of note is the Beckenham Little Theatre. It started life as a play-reading session in the children's section of Beckenham Library in 1948, graduated to actual performances and for a spell leased the H. J. Harvey Memorial Hall. Thanks to the generosity of the builders, Syme and Duncan, and the enthusiasm of Victor Thornton and others it now has its own 47-seater theatre, a converted private house which opened in 1960 at the corner of Manor Road and Bromley Road. It was, until recently, unique in presenting adult plays performed entirely by children. Children grow up and they provide the recruits for the more senior sections of the theatre. Many present day professionals owe their initial training to this modest theatre. Whilst the theatre was using the Harvey Memorial Hall it acquired a bookcase containing a first edition of Holinshed's *History of England* now in the Oxford University Library.

Garages became more opulent and often specialised in a particular make of car. In very recent years they have tended to include convenience shops trading on their drive- in accessibility and long hours, in some cases 24 hours. Because of the increased capital investment required, in many cases they are now either grouped or franchised. Many of the present garage operations in Beckenham now belong to the Masters Group based in Upper Elmers End Road. Its story starts with Ronald Stoneham whose family had a long history of interest in and ownership of cars. They came to the area from New Cross in 1930. Ron acquired a small café in Upper Elmers end Road which was at that time a popular haunt for the drivers on the 536 Highgate to Elmers End route, until it was taken over and extended by the London Passenger Transport Board.

Both he and the shop survived the war and prospered, so much so that he was able to own and race a 500 c.c. Cooper in conjunction with Ken Tyrrell, who was later to make a name for himself in the racing world. Not content with this, for some time he also ran a bookmaking business known as Ron's Ltd. In 1952, sacrificing his racing car, he acquired his first garage, a modest affair called Vincents near *The Rising Sun* public house, which had started as Benn & Vincent's Garage in the 1930s. By dint of long hours and hard work, in 1956 he was able to acquire the Coper's Cope Garage which had been founded by Roderick Selfe as the Albemarle Garage soon after the end of the First World War. In 1963 he moved his headquarters a few yards along the road to the present purpose-built showroom and workshop. Five years later the group acquired the famous Chinese Garage and two years after that Cooter & Green which he renamed Eden Park Continental Cars. Soon after this Ron retired leaving the business in the hands of his son David who, following in his father's footsteps, then acquired the old Saunders & Abbott site in Wickham Road from the Bromley Motor Works and re-named it Autobahn.

Car ownership increased—nowadays 73 per cent of households have access to at least one car compared with the Greater London average of 62.6 per cent. The High Street experiences high levels of traffic movement, congestion and parking contraventions, which are hazardous to pedestrians and motorists alike, and which cause delays in public transport. There are relatively few rear servicing facilities for the High Street shops with virtually none capable of taking the huge articulated and service vehicles which are forced to unload from the street. Public car parking is available in St George's Road which also includes facilities for lorries and coaches. Other car parks are in Fairfield Road behind Christ Church, and in Village Way at Sainsburys. Day-long parking by commuters is at its worst in streets around Beckenham Junction, New Beckenham and Clock House stations.

Regulations for new building developments all have stringent parking standards applied. New houses with four or more bedrooms must have three car spaces per dwelling and those with two-three bedrooms require two spaces. New schools must allow one parking space per member of staff plus 10 per cent for visitors and, where appropriate, for students as well. Cycle stands must be provided. In 1950 not a single member of staff at Marian Vian school went by car but today most senior schools allow their sixth form pupils to drive their own cars. Due to the unreliablity of certain bus services in the area it has become necessary for the council to provide buses for some schoolchildren.

A vacant allotment site at Kangley Bridge was used to provide industrial and warehousing units to create employment for the local population.

Educational changes are still continuing, such as opting out and the new assessment procedures at seven years and 14 years of age. Highfield Primary School and Clare House Primary School have been built in the Shortlands district and Worsley Bridge opened in 1953 to take the junior mixed section from the overcrowded Bromley Road School. The Beckenham Convent school for girls in Foxgrove Road closed in 1988. Langley Park School for Boys, and Langley Park School for Girls have both opted out of the state system as also has Kelsey Park School for Boys.

The lodges at the entrance to the Beckenham Place estate in Southend Road have been made listed buildings as also have three of the original large Victorian houses at the eastern end of Beckenham Place Park Road. These are set amongst dense trees, some of which are the subject of a tree preservation order.

Some of the pressure on the use of the baths was relieved by the provision of the West Wickham baths in 1965, one of the last acts of the Beckenham Council. The final transformation came in 1989 when a leisure centre was grafted on to produce the building as we know it today.

The policy of acquiring open space has continued with the purchase of South Hill Wood, the 10-acre grounds of a large house near the Bromley border, and the much larger Harvington Estate. As Beckenham Place had been acquired by the London County Council as a public open space in 1928, the residents of the town are exceptionally well endowed with recreational space. In fact there can be few towns in the country which have more public parks and open spaces than Beckenham.

Inevitably some aspects of Beckenham have received more attention than others, reflecting to some extent the personal interests of the authors but more often gaps in the record. This is something of which we have become increasingly aware as work on this book went on. Should you be irked by the absence of a reference to something of which you have personal knowledge, we hope you will be encouraged by this account to get in touch with the authors through the publisher. Even better, why not put pen to paper and ensure the preservation of your information by having it published by the Local History Society, whose current address you can obtain from the Local History Section of Bromley Central Library?

Bibliography

Anon, 'St Michael's and All Angels, Souvenir of Completion', 1935

Beaver, P., *The Crystal Palace*, Phillimore, 2nd edn. (1986)

Beckenham Cricket Club Centenary Booklet, 1966

Beckenham Journal

Beckenham Journal Annuals

Beckenham Journal, Diamond Jubilee Supplement, 1936

Beckenham Journal, Centenary Supplement, 1976

Beckenham Lawn Tennis Tournament, Centenary Booklet, 1986

Beckenham & Penge Advertiser

Beckenham & Penge Grammar School 1901-1968

Beckenham Library staff. A brief introduction to the history of Beckenham, Beckenham Libraries (undated)

Beckenham U.D.C. and Borough Council Minutes

Blake, L., *Bromley in the Front Line*, published by the author, 2nd edn. (1983)

Blake, L., *Before the War—A portrait of Bromley & District, 1929-1939*, published by the author (1985)

Borrowman, R., *Beckenham, Past & Present* (1910)

Borough of Beckenham Official Guides

British Red Cross Archives

Bromley Borough Local History Society, various publications

St Michael's & All Angels—Souvenir of Completion 1935

Clark, F. J., *The Story of Christ Church 1876-1926*

Collett, S. W., *Centenary of Beckenham Hospital* (1972)

Copeland, H. Rob., *The Manors of Old Beckenham* (1967)

Copeland, H. Rob., *The Village of Old Beckenham* (1987)

Copeland, H. Rob., *100 years of change in Beckenham* (1974)

Copeland, H. Rob., collection of newspaper cuttings

Godfrey, A., *Old Ordnance Survey Maps*, Anerley & Penge (1868)

Godfrey, A., *Beckenham 1861-71*

Godfrey, A., *Bromley* (1861)

Godfrey, A., *Crystal Palace* (1871)

Godfrey, A., *South Norwood* (1868)

Hasted, E., *The history and topography of Kent 1797*, part III Beckenham & Bromley. pub. Arcturus Press (1985)

Hayes, Miss A. M., *A School at Elmers End*

Hevey, L., *History of Elmers End* and *History of Shortlands*, both published Bromley Borough Local History Society (1991)

Hollmann, H. P., *A Hundred Up, the record of the Club, Beckenham 1884-1984*

Knight & Duffield, *The Story of St Mary's, Shortlands* (1926)

London Research Centre, various articles

Maggs, K., & De Athe P., *The Roman Roads of East Surrey and the Kent Border*, North Downs Press (1987)

Martindale, T. D., *Beckenham & Penge Grammar School 1901-1968*

Morgan, Philip (ed.), *Domesday Book, Kent*, Phillimore (1983)

Motor Sport, various articles

Notley, R., *A guide to St George's Parish Church, Beckenham* (1985)

Porteous, C., *History of Christ Church, 1876-1976*

Pullen, D., *Penge*, published by the author (1990). Contains a complete list of all the remaining legible inscriptions in St George's churchyard, Beckenham.

Somerville-Meikle, J., *St John's, Eden Park 1932-1982*

Syme & Duncan Ltd., 1870-1970

Tonkin, N., *Marian Vian Diamond Jubilee 1932-1992*

Tookey, G. W. Collection

Wagstaff and Pullen (eds.), *Beckenham—an Anthology*, Historical Association. Bromley & Beckenham (1984)

Index

Adams Bros., 12, 69
Alexandra Estate, 19, 52, 70, 83, 93
Alexandra Recreation Ground, 33, 91
Almshouses, 35
Amateur Dramatic Society, 97
Angling, 91
A. R. P., 107
Arthur Road, 53, 85
Assheton Dr., 52
Austin's Pork Shop, 8
Auxiliary Fire Service, 107
Ayling's shoe shop, 67

Bailiff's Cottage, 10
Balfour's Education Act, 55, 63
Balloon Mail, 93
Banks:-
    Barclays, 37
    Lloyds, 37
    Midland, 37, 67
Baron, Joan, 63
Barson, Challoner, 48
Baths, 55, 88, 117, 120
Batten, James, 48
Beckenham Brass Band, 97
Beckenham Lodge, 11, 88
Beckenham Ladies' Swimming Club, 90
Beckenham Men's Swimming Club, 90
Beckenham Motor Co., 48
Beckenham Place, 11, 12, 14, 17, 88, 91, 120, 121
Belgians, 104
Bellrope Field, 53
Beohha, 3
Bevin Boys, 109
Birkbeck Estate, 19, 33, 83
Blacksmith, 47, 65
Blyton, Enid, 59

Boleyn, Anne, 4
Bombs and Rockets, 82, 86, 109, 111
Boots the Chemist, 67, 98
Borrowman, Robert, 1, 8, 12, 23, 31, 34
Bowls, 91
Bowyer, Capt. L., 52
Brandon, Charles, 4
    William, 4
Brett, Sir Piercy, 11
Brewery, 64
Brick making, 65, 110
Brograves, 6, 11
Bruyn, Elizabeth, 4
    Sir Maurice, 3
Burney, Fanny, 12
Burrell, Peter IV, 6
    Sir William, 6
Buses, 46, 54, 110, 119

Cage, The, 27, 34
Cannon Cinema, 98, 117
Castle's Nursery, 69
Cator, Albemarle, 52, 54, 81, 83
    Barwell, 14
    Elizabeth, 14
    John, 4, 11, 12, 14, 23, 52
    Joseph, 11, 14
    Maria, 14
    Mary, 12, 14
    Peter, 14, 17
    William, 37, 81, 82
Cator Estate, 15, 17, 19, 26, 43, 47, 72, 77, 83, 117
Cator Park, 95
Cemetery, 36, 37
Chalmers, Rev. Frederick, 81, 99
Chinese Garage, 8, 10, 23, 51, 109, 120
Choral Society, 97

Christ Church Hospital, 99
Churches:
    All Saints, 83, 86
    Arthur Road Mission, 84
    Avenue Road Mission, 85
    Beckenham Congregational, 85
    Bromley Road Methodist, 85
    Christ Church, 51, 81, 82, 86, 99, 110, 120
    Christ Church Mission Hall, 85
    Christian Witness, 87
    Ebenezer Baptist, 85
    Elmers End Free Church, 85
    Elm Road Baptist, 57, 85
    Goddard Road Congregational, 85
    Holy Trinity, 47, 82, 83
    St Agatha's Chapel, 82
    St Augustine's Mission Hall, 85, 86
    St Barnabas' 82
    St Benedict's, 87
    St Edmund's, 87
    St George's, 19, 27, 36, 39, 76, 77, 81, 86, 104
    St James', 83, 86
    St John's, 85, 86
    St Mary's, 12, 65, 77, 110
    St Michael's & All Angels, 83
    St Paul's, 77
    St Peter's Church Hall, 82
    The Hall, Cromwell Road, 87
Church House, 97, 114
Churchfields Recreation Ground, 91
Cine Society, 97, 119
Clark, G. W., 47, 48
Clock House, 11, 14, 32, 54
Clock House Parade, 54, 65, 67
Cole, Dr. T. Phillip, 63
Collinson, Peter, 12
Copeland, H. Rob., 36, 67, 84
Coper's Cope Farm, 6, 12, 59
Cottage Hospital, 35, 51, 90, 104, 112
Crapper, Thomas, 37
Crease, Ald. James, 95
Crease Park, 6, 95
Cricket, 46, 88, 91
Croydon Road Recreation Ground, 51, 90, 91, 93, 111

Crystal Palace, 1, 14, 27, 29, 34, 36, 69, 81, 89, 91

David Greig's, 73
Davies, J. R., 69
Davis estate, 26
Deen's Garage, 51
De Vere Ltd., 75
Dewhurst's, 67
Domesday Book, 3
Dundas, 6

Eden Farm, 6, 95
Eden, George, 6
    William, 6
Eden Park, 23, 54, 69, 85
Eldorado Ice Cream, 75
Electricity, 31, 36
Elgood Playing Fields, 97
Elm Cottage, 8, 41, 99
Elm Farm, 6
Elmer Lodge, 6, 61
Elmers End, 5, 14, 23, 51, 54, 64, 69, 70, 83, 85, 107
Elwill, Dame Elizabeth, 6
    Sir Edmund, 6
Evacuation, 109
Evans, William, 110
Express Dairy, 73

Fire, 32, 33, 113
Fisher's Education Act, 57
Fleming, Rev. Stewart, 57
Flower Show, 93, 95
Football, 91
Fox, Miss E. M., 57
Foxgrove, John de, 5
Foxgrove Farm, 12, 17
Foxgrove Manor, 5, 6, 11, 23

Gardner, Capt. P. J., 110
Gardner, J. & Co. Ltd., 75, 110
Gas, 29, 34
Gladstone's Education Act, 52, 54
Golf, 12, 23, 91
Goodhart, 6, 19, 23
Gordon House, 8, 11

Grace, W. G., 37
Grosse Smith, Edward, 6
Grote, George, 11, 12
Gwydir, Lord, 6

Hall, The, 11, 59
Harman, L/Cpl. J. P., 110
Harvington Estate, 121
Hayes, Miss, 53
Hearth Tax, 10, 11
Henry VIII, 4
Herbert's Dairy, 73
Hippodrome, 93
Hitt, Frederick, 67
    William, 67
Hitt's Stores, 48, 67
Hoares, 6, 19, 29, 32, 35
Holdstock's Confectionery Shop, 74
Home Guard, 107
Hook's Joinery Works, 75
Horsman's Nursery, 11
Howard's Stores, 48, 67

Ideal Homes Exhibitions, 23
Ironside's Dairy, 73

Jay, The Misses A. J. & W. S., 3
Johnson, Dr., 12

Kelsey Cycle Works, 47
Kelsey Manor, 5, 6, 11, 59, 82, 95
Kelsey Park, 3, 6, 88, 91, 95, 118
Kent House, 1, 6, 8, 12, 47
Kent House Pleasure Gardens, 95
Keston, 3
Kirwan, Rt. Rev. W. H., 87
Kohnstamm, 69

Lace—The Beckenham, 117
Land Army, 109
Langley Chapel, 10
Langley Farm, 6
Langley Lodge, 5, 6, 11, 23
Langley Park Estate, 19, 23, 69, 82
Lea Wilson, Cornelius, 32, 82
    Squire, 19, 26
Linnaeus, 12

Looking Glass Corner, 23

MacFisheries, 67, 116
Malmain, Nicholas, 6
Malyon, William, 72
Manor House, 8, 11, 67, 104
Marks & Spencer, 36, 113
Marsh, Catherine, 81
    Dr., 81
Masters Group, 119
Mathew, Walter Andrew, 73
May Queens, 95
Montague Burton, 26, 67, 116
Moore, Archbishop, 6
    Dr., 3
Muirhead's, 35, 36, 69, 70, 98, 110

Nichols, Doris, 63
Nitty Norah, 63
Noah's Ark, 46
Norwood, Lt. J., 59, 110

Oakwood, 102
Odeon Cinema, 98
Odo, 3
Old Manor House, 11, 12, 29, 32, 97
Old Wood House, 8, 47
Orchestral Society, 97
Ousley's Dairy, 54, 73
Overton's Dairy, 73

Padbury's, 47
Pavilion Cinema, 8, 98
Payne's Jewellers, 73
Pearce, chimney sweep, 73
Peek, Francis, 82
    Lydia, 83
Percy Jones & Co., 70
Peters, William, 12
Photographic Society, 97
Pillin, John, 47, 51
Pitt, 6, 65
Police, 32
Poll Tax, 10, 11
Pooley, Father, 87
Porcupine Field, 19
Post, 39, 93
Price's Bedding Factory, 48

Prudential Assurance Co., 14
Public Houses:-
   Eden Park Hotel, 63
   George Inn, The, 8, 11, 34, 48, 73, 97
   Greyhound, The, 117
   Oakhill Tavern, 46
   Rising Sun, 23, 120
   Three Tuns, The, 6, 8, 32, 41, 88
   William IV, 23, 48

Railways, 41, 43, 81
Railway Hotel, 46, 48
Raymond, Amy, 6
   Hugh, 6
   Jones, 6
Rectory, 11, 31, 67, 97
Red Cross, 57, 99
Regal Cinema, 98, 117
Retford—Robt. de, 5
Reynolds, Sir Joshua, 12
Ritson, Rev. C. J., 83
River Beck, 1, 3, 11
   Chaffinch, 1, 54
   Pool, 1
Rokele, Matilda, 3
   Sir Richard, 6
Romans, 1, 3

Safeway's, 73, 116
Sainsbury, J. plc., 8, 67, 75, 116, 120
St Arvan's, 55
St Bride's House, 114
St John, Sir Oliver, 4
Saunders & Abbott, 33, 47, 48, 120
Schools:-
   Abbey, 59
   Albemarle College, 61
   Alexandra, 53, 57
   Balgowan, 57, 99
   Beckenham & Penge County, 55
   Bishop Challoner, 61
   Bromley Road, 52, 57, 104, 120
   Cator Park, 57
   Churchfields, 53
   Clare House, 61
   Clare House Primary, 120
   Craven College, 61

   Grange Preparatory, 61
   Highfield, 120
   Kelsey Park Boys, 57, 120
   Kentwood, 57
   Kepplestone, 59
   Langley Park Boys, 55, 120
   Langley Park Girls, 120
   Lennard Road County, 57, 99
   Marian Vian, 23, 53, 57, 120
   Minshull House, 58, 59
   Raymont, 59
   Royal Academy of Dancing, 63
   Royston, 57
   St Christopher's, 59
   St James', 53
   St Olaf's, 62
   School of Art, 54, 62
   Stewart Fleming, 57
   Technical Institute, 54, 55, 86
   Woodbrook, 62
   Worsley Bridge, 120
Scouts, 55
Shortlands, 17, 33, 34, 46, 72
Shortlands House, 11, 12, 17, 61, 77
Simons, W. L., 74
Siren Motor Works, 48
Sisleys, 75
Sloane Hospital, 113
Small Electric Motors, 69, 70
Smith & Haydn, 75
Smith, W. H. Ltd., 8, 26, 98
South Hill Wood, 121
South Suburban Co-Op, 73
Stanhope Grove, 23, 95
Stanmar Products, 75
Stations:-
   Beckenham Junction, 23, 41, 114, 120
   Birkbeck, 41
   Clock House, 6, 41, 120
   Elmers End, 41, 54
   Kent House, 41
   New Beckenham, 41, 84, 120
   Penge East, 19, 41
   Ravensbourne, 114
   Shortlands, 41, 77
Stone Farm, 6, 8
Stoneham, Ron., 119, 120

Style, Humphrey, 6
    John, 6
Swimming, 55
Syme & Duncan, 65, 77, 119

Taylor's, 19, 23, 26
Teignmouth, Lord, 6
Telephones, 36
Tennis, 23, 89
Tesco's, 116
Thayers Farm, 6
Thornton Hedley, 104
    Stanley, 104
    Thomas, 72, 118
    Victor, 73, 118, 119
Thornton's Corner, 14, 19, 43, 51
Thrale, Mrs., 12
Tillings Bus, 46
Toll Gates, 47
Tonard Brazing Co. Ltd., 73
Tootswood, 1, 3, 17
Tostevin, J. W., 47
Trams, 43
Twinlocks, 69, 70

United Dairies, 73

Vansittart, 6

Victoria Cross, 59, 110
Village Place, 11, 19, 26, 32, 69
Vincents, 120
Violetts, 6

Wall's Ice Cream, 75
War Memorial, Beckenham, 51, 104, 117
    Shortlands, 104
Water, 29, 34
Watson, Mary, 52
Weeks, 67
Welch, William, 81, 82
Wellcome Foundation, 23, 70
Westminster, Duke of, 19
Whitfield Daukes, Rev. S., 83
Wilberforce, 6
Wilkinson, W. A., 12, 17, 19, 26, 77
Wilson, Alderman, 32, 82
Wolseley, 37
Woodbastwick Hall, 12, 14
Woolworths, 26, 67
Workhouse, 31, 52
Wurlitzer Organ, 98, 117
Wytecroft, Richard de, 23

Y.M.C.A., 87, 104

Zeppelin, 109

Plan of an Estate
AT
BECKENHAM,
IN THE COUNTY OF
KENT,
THE PROPERTY OF
Albemarle Cator, Esqᵣᵉ.
NOVEMBER 1864.

Note - The Boundary of the Estate is coloured Green.
The Land coloured Pink is Let.

SCALES.

Mid Kent and
Addiscombe Railways ———— Blue
W. End and Crystal Palace
now L.C.&D. Rᵈ ———— Red
London Chatham & Dover Rᵈ ———— Yellow